FLIPPING HOUSES

Comprehensive Beginner's Guide to Buying and Selling Houses

TABLE OF CONTENTS

Introduction 1

CHAPTER 1: The Immeasurable Value of Immovable Property 5

A Sneak Peek at the Prospects 6

Why Not Start a Business? 7

Why Not Build and Sell? 11

Are There Risks? 14

Why You Should Go Through With It Anyway 15

CHAPTER 2: Finding a Flip-Worthy Home 18

What Makes a Good Investment? 19

Single-Family vs Multi-Family Units 30

It's All in the Timing - When to Buy a Property 32

Establishing Your Timetable 34

Decisions, Decisions - Where to Find a Flipping House 37

Funding Your Fix N' Flip 44

CHAPTER 3: Real Transformation Through Renovation 48

The Foundations of a Cost-Effective Renovation 49

The 4 Kinds of Home Renovations 55

Putting Together Your Dream Team 58

Smart Tips for Renovating a Flip 61

Establishing the Cost of Renovation 66

How to Stay on Schedule 68

CHAPTER 4: From Fix to Flip
- Putting Your Property on the Market **73**

Different Methods of Selling a Home.. 74

Setting the Stage - How to Stage Your House for Sale.................. 78

Establishing Your After Repair Value 82

The Cost of Temporary Ownership 85

Negotiating a Sale... 88

When There Aren't Any Bites... 91

CHAPTER 5: Other Ways to Liquidate or Profit Off a Flip **99**

When It's Time for Plan B.. 100

Exit Strategies for a Potential Flop 102

CHAPTER 6: The Makings of a Flop
- Common Mistakes to Avoid **107**

Choosing the Wrong House... 108

Ignoring the Neighbors.. 109

Paying Too Much 109

Poor Renovation Choices 110

Overlooking Permits and Fees.. 111

Miscalculating Holding Fees... 112

Using Standard Smartphones for Pictures 112

Not Posting Enough 113

Fitting Everything Into an Unreasonable Timetable 114

Pushing Plan A 114

Paying Full for Materials.. 115

Avoiding the Experts 116

Underestimating Staging 116

Thinking It's a One-Man Job 117

Spitballing the ARV 118

Doing Eraser Math 119

Making Your Savings a Part of the Equation 119

Forgetting the Buyers 120

Believing Too Strongly In Your Property.......................121

Losing Sight of Time..122

Conclusion...**124**

Introduction

"Now, one thing I tell everyone is learn about real estate.
Repeat after me: real estate provides the highest returns, the
greatest values, and the least risk."

- Armstrong Williams

So, maybe you just inherited a fortune from the untimely passing of an obscure aunt. Maybe you struck gold and found yourself staring at the winning PowerBall ticket right there in your hands. Maybe you actually broke your back trying to build that 6 or 7-digit bank account you've been working hard on for years. Whatever the case, you've got some green to spend. So you just gotta ask - what should you spend it on?

Any Tom, Dick, or Harry would probably run down to the nearest car dealership and sign the papers to a sweet new cherry red sports car. But not you. You're a smart guy (or gal!) and you know that the best way to spend money is to spend it on things that make money.

If you're traveling down that road, you'll find that there are over a thousand business ventures you can dive right into. You can franchise a restaurant, start a clothing line, invest in stocks, open up a bed and breakfast, build the next big super-gym! Really, the options are endless. But are they as profitable and promising as they seem?

1

According to statistics released by Bloomberg, 8 out of 10 businesses crash and burn within the first 18 months of operation. Within that time, an entrepreneur might have spent every last penny of his resources or savings in order to try to keep his burning ship afloat.

Unfortunately, starting a business is rarely as easy as it seems, even if you manage to attend as many Michael E. Gerber talks as possible. It takes talent, guts, and courage to be able to make something so risky and initially unstable to work and actually keep running for years down the line.

If that isn't reason enough for you to seek other profitable ventures, you should know that opening up a business can be particularly taxing over time. All that bookkeeping, managing, taking inventories, updating your store's facade, training new employees, mitigating employee issues, setting up a marketing plan, executing said plan, taking care of customers, making sure they're happy after they've transacted with your store, and trying to rake in new buyers and clients to bump up sales - all for the foreseeable future. Whew!

Considering the fact that this isn't even an all exhaustive list makes you wonder why some people think that opening up a business can be a sideline opportunity for passive income. Quite the contrary, when you start up a venture, you need to quit your day job and sacrifice personal hours to make sure you don't end up as one of the 8 failed businesses out of 10.

Okay, so what about stocks? Unless you've got the makings of the next Paul Tudor Jones, you might be better off taking your money elsewhere. Trading stocks is immensely technical, and investing in stable stocks could mean it might take years before you can cash out your first thousand dollars of profit. So unless you're willing to wait that long or study that hard, you might want to steer clear of stock trading for the time being.

Now, what option does that leave you? What about… real estate? Before you raise a brow and say that investing in property is the opposite of your idea of an "exciting financial venture," you should know that some of the world's richest have made their millions through intuitive real estate strategies. Take the controversial President Donald Trump's words for it:

"It's tangible, it's solid, it's beautiful, it's artistic from my standpoint, and I just **love** real estate!"

Sure, not everyone might agree with Trump's radical political decisions as president, but nearly everyone will admit that he isn't wrong when it comes to his passion for real estate. There are lots of ways to make money off of real estate, and contrary to popular belief, it can be very exciting. For instance, take house flipping.

Considered by many as an extreme real estate sport, house flipping is a fast-paced investment strategy that takes what you have and doubles it over the span of 1 year. If you can liquidate in less time, then you've made a faster ROI than you probably would have in 3 years of operating the most successful restaurant franchise you could find.

Taking an old house, sprucing it up, and flipping it over to sell it at a higher price can make you millions in the shortest possible time, but that isn't even the best part. Unlike stock trading which can get technical and entrepreneurship which can be immensely tiring and demanding, flipping houses is easy to learn and non-intensive.

Does that mean that anyone can just dive right in and make it work? Relative to a lot of other ventures out there, house flipping can be easy as pie - as long as you take the time to actually study and learn it. Hey, no one becomes an expert just because they really, really want to be.

Fortunately however, learning the ins and outs of real estate can be a whole lot less complicated, especially if you've got a guide like this one.

If you're ready to discover your ticket to making millions, if you want to grow those stagnant funds, and if you want to have it all with the least risk and most potential gain, then keep on reading as we steer you through the wonderfully exciting world of house flipping.

CHAPTER

1

The Immeasurable Value
of Immovable Property

*"Real estate cannot be stolen, nor can it be carried away.
Purchased with common sense, paid for in full, and
managed with reasonable care, it is about the safest
investment in the world."*

- Franklin D. Roosevelt

A Sneak Peek at the Prospects

Fortunately for you, the younger adult generations have their eyes set on *other* riches - like experience! If you haven't noticed it yet by scanning your social media feeds, you'll notice that most millennials and even quite a few of those from Generation X before them are more *invested* in things like travel and experience. So the immovable property market has hit quite a bit of a standstill since they took over the majority of the workforce.

Back in the day, life was simpler and individual human goals and ambitions were far more traditional, driving people to make financial decisions that leaned more towards *domestication*. That's why the baby boomers - probably your parents - were able to declare *the security of home ownership* in their late 20's or early 30's. These days however, adult minds are geared towards much less *permanent* "investments."

According to studies, millennials are far less prepared or interested to purchase properties because they're more inclined to *see the world* and spend money on travel. Technology, fashion, and luxury items rank next as the highest on the millennials' list of essentials, so living with mom and dad for a few extra years doesn't seem like such a bad strategy for cutting costs.

What's more, it seems millennials are tying the knot far later than their boomer counterparts. With more of these young adults pushing the marrying age towards their mid-30's, the *necessity* of buying a home doesn't spark their interest until they've decided to settle down with their partner later in life.

So why should any of this be beneficial to you, oh, humble house flipper? According to statistics, the demand for real estate properties will boom in about 5 years - when all of those millennials finally decide that it's time to make some *real* investments.

But between now and then, the property market has hit an all-time post-recession low because of the trend towards renting instead of buying. For you, this means there are far more choices and less competition when it comes to scouting potential investments.

But there's more promise in store for those who have the courage to flip properties. Experts foresee that millennials will *soon* realize the need to purchase, and that increase in demand is likely to occur within the next 5 to 10 years when these individuals discover the benefit of owning a house and achieve the financial capability in order to secure their own home. So *at this very point in time*, you're essentially one step ahead of everyone else.

Why Not Start a Business?

A difficult debate for most people who find the burning desire to *make more* is whether to start a business or to invest in real estate. No doubt, both prospects have their own pros and cons, and for every person who has taken on house flipping, there are probably a thousand others who decided to venture into business ownership.

So why might it not be for you? Consider the downsides.

They're Fickle

Unlike houses - which are a *necessity all year round* - businesses tend to have seasons. For instance, ice cream shops get more customers at around summertime, with very few patrons during cold weather. This means you'd have to factor in the down season to offset your expenses while the sun shines.

The problem? Trends won't always be the same. So while you might be able to establish some semblance of a pattern over the span of 2 years, things can change over your third year. This is especially true if a competitor with pumped up offers and better facilities pops up next door, which can pretty much mess up your projections altogether.

Finding a Niche is Hard

You can't just *decide* on a business venture and be done with it. Most owners find that it's *imperative* to perform research in order to identify the gaps in a market. Sometimes, it's not gaps, but market preferences. What do patrons want to see? What do they like?

Once you travel down that road, you'll find that there are a plethora of factors you probably hadn't considered when the thought of business ownership first popped into your head. These include the scale of your enterprise, the specific products and services you need to offer, and how you might spice up your business framework to set yourself apart from the competition.

On top of that, you need to understand your market. Who wants to buy your product? Who needs your services? How old are they, where do they live, and how might they try to look for a business like yours?

Studying your target audience in depth is a vital part of understanding how to go about building your identity. So, no, the idea that you just get to choose *whatever your heart desires* when starting a business can be total bull - it's all about pleasing customers.

What happens if you get the market wrong? Well, that's how businesses fail. Yikes.

They're Cost and Time Intensive

Probably the most difficult part about owning a business - and a factor that most hopefuls tend to overlook – is that they eat up quite a bit of time and money. Just like a newborn baby, a fresh business concept needs *most,* if not all, of your time and attention. It needs you to keep an eye on all operations because success depends on it.

Aside from requiring a large chunk of your waking hours, businesses also need a whole lot of green. The less money you have to spare, the less appealing your start-up might seem to consumers. Of course, you can improve later on once you make a little profit, but don't expect any too soon.

The reality of owning a business is that for the first how many months, *you will not make a profit.* Harsh reality, but true nonetheless. It will take time for your business to pick up, and during those first few months after you let your little venture walk on its own two feet, you'll have to call the right shots to draw in customers.

So, who pays for the utilities, the employee salaries and benefits, the loan amortization for equipment and furniture that you might have purchased, rent, and other overhead expenses? You, of course. The longer it takes you to make a profit, the longer you'll find yourself having to pay for everything out of your own pocket.

Surely, once the cashflow starts to normalize, you won't have to dig deep into your own pockets anymore, right? Wrong. Some months might see more sales than others, and some months might give you negative numbers.

So most of the profit you make should have to be saved for a rainy day. If you're expecting a downward turn in cash-in next month, any profit you make today should have to be set aside to offset your overhead next month.

It's a difficult and often confusing balancing act, and unless you've got the time for it, a business can be *incredibly prone* to losses.

What Investment?

Some hopefuls think that buying equipment for a business is considered an *investment*, but one of the basic cornerstones of the idea of an 'investment' is transferability. It has to be versatile and adaptable - with indispensable value even in the context of a different niche.

So unless there are other uses for that 6-station rotary screen printing machine aside from making, well, prints, then no, it's not exactly an investment. If your business goes downhill and you decide it's time to liquidate, you're not likely to be able to sell your screen printing machine at full cost, causing you to incur losses.

With business ownership, the only real 'investment' you can have is your brand. Successful brands become franchise-worthy, which essentially means that people are willing to pay to have their own branch of your enterprise. You offer the business model, they finance the capital expenditure and overhead, and you get royalties from their sales.

What are some of the businesses that offer franchising? McDonald's, 7/Eleven, and Subway, for example. What do they have in common? They're all *iconic.* For hopefuls, it could take decades, and perhaps even a lifetime to establish the same popularity.

So even if you've had a successful run over the past few years, if you're not well-established enough to sell franchises, they your only option to make more money off of your brand would be to sell it to someone else altogether. This means giving up your ownership and losing any rights to the business you worked hard to build.

Why Not Build and Sell?

So, *why flipping?* Why not just buy land, build something spectacular on it, and sell that instead? Surely, it's *easier* to design something that's *beautiful right off the bat* instead of trying to wrestle with the ugly demons of a run-down mid-century house.

Quite the contrary, *there's a lot of money to be made on run-down houses.* For instance, foreclosed properties can cost as much as 37% less than similarly located homes. Sure, flipping a foreclosure might be an entirely different challenge all on its own, but for the savvy real estate property pro, it can be even more profitable since the initial cost to acquire the property is so low.

There are a few other reasons why you might want to consider buying old houses and flipping them for a profit as opposed to building and selling.

They're Usually Cheaper

Depending on the area where you're operating, you might find that old properties can cost twice or three times less than building from scratch. For instance, you might find a home worth $115,000 USD, pour a couple thousand to give it some appeal, and flip it for $225,00 USD.

As opposed to buying land and building, that can be a much lower entry point, allowing you to enjoy the benefits of property investing without the need to shell out such a large amount. What makes building expensive?

Labor and the cost of materials are at an all-time high, making them inaccessible to most investment hopefuls. This is especially true if you don't really have much to go on, limiting your options and possibly sacrificing the build quality of the home you develop because of a shortage of funds.

They're Faster

It's not called house "flipping" for no reason. The process of buying a built house, renovating it, and putting it back up on the market in a few months' time can be *lightning fast* which bids well for your ROI. Most house flippers hold on to properties for just a few short months, or a maximum of a year.

According to ATTOM Data Solutions, the average profit made on a flip during the 3rd quarter of 2017 in the United States was $66,448. Assuming this was all done in the span of 6 months means you could make over $130,000 USD in one year. That's *if* you're only flipping one house at a time.

With build and sells, it could take more than a year before you manage to bring your listing to the public. With the tedious process of securing building permits, and the inevitable construction hiccups, you might not be able to make the same kind of ROI if you're building from the ground up.

They Can Be More Profitable

There are a lot of factors that contribute to the profitability of a flipped house. Timing, location, competition, build quality, demand, interest rates, and yes - even the history of the property you've chosen can all have a big impact on the amount of money you can make off of it.

Despite all these though, a flipper who manages to get things right can reap the benefit of an exceptionally handsome profit. So much so that he might even make more compared to a building and selling a brand-new house.

Of course, things can change, and circumstances are always different. But generally speaking, most *investment* minded individuals - and successful investors at that - lean more towards flipping than building and selling because it can be significantly more rewarding even after just a short period of time.

Are There Risks?

There is no such thing as a perfect business venture or investment. So you need to anticipate that there will *always* be risks that could stem from your own mistakes or from the nature of the venture itself. With that, you might be asking - *what's the catch* with house flipping?

The Flip Might Flop

There are lots of house flipping horror stories of investors failing to make profit within the ideal time frame. With such an unpredictable market, there really is no way to determine whether you'd be able to make a sale, even after you follow all the right steps.

If you can't sell the house soon after it's done with renovations and if you didn't buy it in full, then you'd have to continue paying the mortgage from your own pocket until it catches the interest of a sure buyer. This - called the holding cost - is a major risk that can easily give any investor a string of endless headaches.

Property Unpredictability

It's commonplace for flippers to find possible investments in foreclosures and auctions. At these events, you get the opportunity to purchase for exceptionally low prices, making it an ideal method for securing a suitable house for a small capital expenditure.

The downside? Buying from an auction means you won't have the opportunity to fully inspect the house before purchase. While it might look decent and well-built at a glance, closer examination may reveal significant damages that can significantly bump up renovation and repair costs.

Fault foundations, mold and mildew, and the need for a complete plumbing restoration and repair could mean that you'll end up spending much more on renovations than you would gain after sales.

Expecting the Unexpected

Unfortunately, this is one thing that house flipping has in common with entrepreneurship. While brushing up on the latest real estate news can help you establish a trend, the reality is that the real estate market can change in the blink of an eye.

Other than that, renovations can also give you a few jump scares. Running behind deadlines, underestimating the work it would take to completely restore a fixer-upper, and encountering more than a few hiccups throughout the process can have you grinding your teeth as you lose profit over days spent handling and renovating a property.

Why You Should Go Through With It Anyway

Hey, you didn't sign up to fail and no one wants to deal with the dangers of losing hard-earned cash on a venture that won't thrive. But you've got to remember - *success is very possible* if you make sure that you play your cards right. Any business opportunity or investment prospect comes with its own, unique set of dangers and possible losses, but if you don't dive in and try out in the first place, you'll never get the chance at success.

If you're wondering whether a property investment really is the right choice for you, consider some of the generic benefits of buying real estate in the first place:

Demand Will Always Be Around

Okay, so maybe you decided to put your investment on the market at the wrong time and now it's just sitting there, waiting for buyers that don't even seem to exist.

Although no flipper wants to lose time hoping to get a nibble on property advertisements, you have to remember that houses will always have demand. Regardless of how dismal the market might seem at any given point, *there will always be people looking for houses because there will always be people who need houses!*

Give it a few years, and that dreary immovable property market can significantly soar and give you a line of hungry house hunters just waiting to call first dibs on your place. Of course, if you find that you might have a hard time selling after you're done with renovations, you can always turn to rentals.

In our modern day and age when young adults are more interested in other expenses, properties take a back seat. So any millennial would be happy to rent because it gives them more freedom and less commitment. If you end up deciding to rent your space out, you could possibly prop it up at the cost of your monthly mortgage to off-set the holding cost and keep you at break-even.

Prices Will Keep Increasing

A trend that we've seen year in and year out gives property investors the peace of mind knowing that they've chosen the right assets to spend their money on. And that trend is the steady, reliable increase of house prices over time. Over the last decade, the property market in the United States has seen a steady rise in real estate costs and is even anticipated to increase twice as much in the coming years.

What this means for flippers is that although there is the real risk of not being able to liquidate as quickly as 6 months to a year, there will always be the guarantee that prices will inflate as the years roll on. So even if you can't sell it *today*, you can sell for more *tomorrow* so you can cut back on your losses.

It's as REAL as It Gets

The inherent beauty of real estate is that, well - *it's real!* You can't corrupt it, it can't be stolen, it doesn't shrink over time, it doesn't perish, and it's permanent. So unlike other investments like cars which depreciate over time, or gold which is prone to theft or loss, *immovable properties* are fixed so you can be sure that what you had tomorrow is what you will have today.

The tides may turn and seasons may change, and you might not be able to liquidate when you want to. But as long as you've got your name on that title, you will be in possession of a very real, incorruptible investment that adds a significant notch to your net worth.

Finding a Flip-Worthy Home

"Buy real estate in areas where the path exists and buy more real estate where there is no path but where you can create your own."

- David Waronker

The foundation of an efficient flip is an ideal home, and the asset of a successful property investor is the capacity to *see* the possibilities in a house that might only seem run-down and dilapidated to many of the others who lay eyes on it.

For beginners, there might only be two ways of seeing potential flips - the first is *too risky* and the second is *too easy*. Don't worry - everyone started out looking through the same two-toned glasses. But you can hone your eye for investment to break through the initial impression and see what's *really* there.

What Makes a Good Investment?

Not every house you see will translate to an easy sale, and not all of them will flop. As an investor, you need to understand that there are *intrinsic* factors that add to the saleability of a house, and that the future of your investment doesn't solely rely on your capacity to mitigate risks and avoid mistakes.

So what are some of the factors you can use to determine whether or not a potential property will make you the profits you want?

Location, Location, Location

A basic principle of property investment that's often considered a no-brainer is *location*. Is the house in a safe locality? Is it near key points in the community like grocery stores, hospitals, and schools? Is it easy to get to and from the property by car? Are there any other methods of transport that could make it possible for a homeowner and his family to access the home with as little stress and effort as possible? Is it located on a busy main road? Does it get passed by lots of traffic? Or is it quiet and secluded? What about privacy? What about the neighborhood?

Location is a key factor in saleability because it tells your buyers whether this is a place where *they can grow some roots*. Individuals seeking to purchase immovable property with the purpose of *living in it* want to make sure they'd get to enjoy the convenience of living in a place that suits their lifestyle.

And because most of those with the capacity to purchase are older adults who have settled down with a partner and are possibly planning to start a small family, a location in a quiet suburban setting or something similar can be incredibly promising for a flipper.

All of that said, you might want to look out for warning signs that may make it difficult for you to liquidate your investment even after intensive renovations.

- Clogged up streets where lots of cars might be parked such as those near churches or gas stations

- Houses that are located around the periphery of commercial establishments like convenience stores

- Properties in largely commercial localities with very few other houses around it (commonly seen as "unsafe")

- Houses in polluted areas with lots of noise, smoke, and littered garbage

- Areas where there have been consistent reports of break-ins and security threats

- Houses which are *too far* from key points in the community

- Those in areas where there has been a steady decline in property value

Ensuring that your chosen property is nestled in a location that's ideal to buyers will significantly improve your chances of making a sale. On top of that, choosing the right location also helps guarantee that your property will always have an increasing market value regardless of whether or not you have potential buyers at the moment. So even if you bulldoze that house completely and decide to do something else with your land, you can be sure that you won't lose your investment's inherent potential to *make you a profit.*

But there's *more* to deciding on location than simply ticking items off of a pre-determined list. When scouting properties, your choice of location becomes more dynamic when you consider the kind of purchaser you might encounter for that *specific* home given the context that it sits in.

Check the surroundings - are most of the residents single office workers? Then you might not actually need to consider the presence of a school within the vicinity. If the location caters more to families, then you should make sure you're within a reasonable distance to some educational institutions.

Do most of the people in the neighborhood get around in private cars? If not, then you best make sure your chosen home is accessible to public transport. If it isn't on the daily bus route, does it at least have a driveway or garage where your buyer can safely keep their car?

The best way to ascertain that you're making the right choice would be to consider *yourself* living at your chosen location. What kind of buyer would feel comfortable in this type of locality? What would they look for? And what features would be important to them? The power of being able to put yourself into a prospective homeowner's shoes provides incredible insight as to the potential of your property investment.

Physical Characteristics

Here's where making the choice might become a little more confusing. The *physical characteristics* of the property will play a major role in profit because that's *all you have to go on* in terms of how far you can flip your property.

Remember, unless you're willing to cut back on your profit just so you can spend more on bigger, more extensive renovations, the smarter choice would be to spend as little on repairs as possible while generating the most positive change. So what your chosen property brings to the table is essentially what it will look like after the renovations are done - with a few improvements of course.

That said, you should be capable of seeing potential even if it doesn't really look like such a great space to begin with. A lot of the most successful flips are those that entail quite a lot of *cosmetic* changes, meaning that the houses didn't really look too impressive to start.

If you detect some structural damage though, tread lightly. More experienced flippers would be better suited to handle such properties since they can require quite a bit of expertise. Plus, if the problems go beyond carpet deep, then you might be staring down the front end of a costly investment flop.

How do you figure out if a house is worth flipping based on appearances? Here's a short guide to help you make the right choice:

- Seamless transition from space to space (There aren't any rooms that you can only enter by going through another room, with the exception of a master bath)

- Reasonable ratio of bedrooms to bathrooms (Some houses can have 4 bedrooms and just 1 bathroom, making it inconvenient for large families)

- High ceilings and lots of free-flowing air (Lower ceilings tend to make spaces feel cramped and tight, which doesn't rub well with most buyers)

- Updated floor plan (Some houses that were built in specific decades might resonate with that time frame's aesthetic and design trends, making them feel outdated and old even after renovations)

- Versatility of space (Rooms that can be used as bedrooms can be easily converted to dens and offices should the homeowner see it fit)

Some can be very deceiving, but the general aesthetic of the houses around it can give you a clue. So try to check out the competition - what do the other houses for sale in the neighborhood look like?

This should also tell you *how big a house* you should invest in. The average size of houses in the area is the sweet spot you want to aim for. Anything cheaper might require that you make price adjustments that could work against your profit. Anything more expensive could mean that you'd have to wait longer for anyone to take interest in your investment.

If most of the houses for sale in the area are 2 bedroom, 2 toilet and baths, then you need to have at least those same features. If they're mostly 1500 square foot properties, you need to land within that average land size. This just helps keep you in line with competition.

However, there are some instances when you might call a few shots that don't necessarily fit this algorithm. For instance, one house flipper noticed that in a neighborhood with houses that cost between $250,000 - $400,000 USD, the smaller houses for sale would almost always get snapped up instantly, leaving the average-sized and larger lots on the market for a longer time.

The reason was because it was a very nice community that catered to small families with young children. There was also a nearby school that was considered one of the best for preschoolers.

All of these factors worked to make the smallest houses sell because families would be happy to simply *be* in that specific locality. Because most of these homeowners were just starting out and because they wanted to expose their kids to the best possible environment, they would gladly settle for the lower end properties.

So while all the information listed above might start you off on the right track, keep in mind that you should make judgment on a case to case basis, especially once you learn how to tie all the factors together.

Expenditures and Potential Profit

The good news is that diving into fix and flips can be extremely lucrative. The bad news is that you need to actually do the math in order to find out whether or not there's any profit in a house you've chosen.

While there's a completely separate, in-depth discussion on computations later on, it's important to get this information out of the way at this point just to give you a fuller understanding of the *factors* that make up a good purchase. For now, we'll focus on the basic *financial terms* that you need to wrap your head around so that the rest of this guide makes sense.

- **Purchase Price** - the initial cost it would take to acquire the property. If you're buying in cash, it's the full market value of the property plus any fees required to finalize and close the purchase. If you're borrowing from a lender, it's the cost of the down payment plus any added fees.

- **Rehabilitation Cost** - the amount needed in order to fully renovate and restore the house prior to be placed on the market for sale. This includes any cosmetic repairs as well as structural renovations.

- **Holding Cost** - in case of a mortgaged property, this is the amount the investor would have to pay in order to maintain the property under his or her name. Monthly mortgage payments need to be paid in order to prevent the house from being repossessed by the bank. Until a buyer takes interest in the property and decides to purchase, the investor would have to continue the mortgage payments to prevent repossession or foreclosure.

- **Cash on Cash Return** - measures the amount of cash profit earned on the cash spent to acquire, restore, and flip a real estate property.

- **Return on Investment** - this performance measure is used to determine the amount of profit made on an investment. The higher the ROI, the more money you made given the amount you spend to complete the venture.

- **After Repair Value** - the cost the house might sell for once all of the repairs are completed.

Well, wasn't that a mouthful? There are a whole lot of other terms to learn down the line, but for now, we'll work with this short list. Essentially, you'll want to have a rough estimate of the profit you'd make off of a property based on the initial numbers you're presented.

Keep in mind though that your financial considerations will change depending on whether you plan to rent out the property or to flip it all together to make a quick sale. As a general rule, rentals should provide you a stream of income over time enough to restore your initial cash out within a given period. With complete flips, you should be able to generate a suitable profit as soon as the property is ready to be sold.

The difficulty with assessing a property's potential for profit is that there is no *sure way* to accurately come up with the numbers. Sure, you can always crunch the computations, calculate the costs, and make projections based on market trends. But in essence, all the math would be speculative because the circumstances today might not be the circumstances tomorrow.

So how can you calculate the potential profit you can make off of a property at a glance? Take the house cost, add the cost of renovation, and add about another 15-20% of the market value of the house at acquisition to cover other fees and charges associated with your investment. Then check the vicinity for other houses for sale that have similar qualities to the one you're buying. How much do they sell for?

Subtracting the total expenses from the selling price of similar homes will give you an idea as to how much you can make off of the property once you make the sale. Is it worth the trouble and the time? Remember, in 2017 house flippers would make an average of $66,000 USD on a single flip which was considered ideal. Of course, the amount you'd make will change depend on the qualities of the property you're selling.

Generally speaking though, an investor should be looking to make anywhere between 10% - 20% ROI on a property. So regardless of the cost of the property and its qualities, you should be seeking to make a return that comes to around 10% or 20%.

So how do you compute the ROI at the start to find out whether a house is worth the flip? Take this simple computation into consideration:

$$\frac{\textit{Net Profit}}{\textit{Total expense}} \times \textbf{100\%}$$

If for example, you expect to make $40,000 off the sale of a house that cost you $200,000 to acquire and repair, your ROI would be 20% which is actually a very impressive estimation.

Again, a lot of the math can be speculative no matter how solid the numbers might seem at a glance. To be able to formulate an accurate ROI before you even make an offer on the house, you need to come up with the most accurate estimations as possible.

Consider the cost of the house and add anywhere between 10%-20% to cover any additional fees to finalize the purchase. Then, make an estimate of the renovation costs based on what you see upon inspection. This is typically 10% of the purchase price. Add all of that together and you have your *total expense*.

To figure out how much you can make off of the house, consider similar properties in the neighborhood. Make sure to scout options of relatively the same price and physical properties (ie. Number of bedrooms, bathrooms, other features, quality of finishes, general "newness," etc.)

How much are they selling for? Will your property look the same way, or will your renovations make your house look more appealing? If so, how much do you think you can price your *improved* property versus these other listings in the area?

So, to put all of that into perspective, consider a $300,000 USD property with 3 bedrooms, 2 toilet and baths, and a 2 car garage and add around 15% to cover purchase fees, which would be around $45,000 USD. Now, consider the cost of renovation which would be 10% of the purchase price - $30,000 USD. All things considered, you'd have to pay a total of $375,000 to acquire the property, pay for the fees of purchase, and have the house renovated.

Around the area, you notice that other 3BR/2TB properties are selling for around $420,000 - $470,000 USD. Just to keep your price competitive, you set your selling price at $450,000 USD. Now, you can compute your ROI.

Total Expenses = $300,000 + $45,000 + $30,000 = $375,000

Net Profit = $450,000 - $375,000 = $75,000

$$\frac{\$75,000}{\$375,000} \times 100\% = 20\%$$

Is it too optimistic? It might be. Are there other factors that could affect the profit you make? Absolutely. Holding costs will have to be paid from your own pocket until someone decides to purchase the property from you. These include taxes, utilities, and possibly the mortgage if you purchased with the help of a lender.

The 70% Rule

When flipping properties, you'll come across a principle called the 70% Rule. This states that an investor shouldn't pay more than 70% of the after repair value of a property minus the cost of renovation in order to acquire the house. In essence, the purpose of the 70% Rule is to guarantee that you don't pay *more than you can afford* in order to purchase a house. It also helps ensure that you'd make a reasonable profit off of your investment.

How do you compute ARV? Before making the purchase, there really is no way to know for sure. Your best bet would be to check out surrounding houses for sale of a similar quality, build, and size. How much are they selling for? That should give you an idea as to how much you can get for a property once you renovate it.

Now that you have a rough estimate, you can compute with the 70% Rule.

Cost of acquisition = ARV x 70% - cost of renovation

If you expect to sell a house for around $225,000 USD after it's repaired, and you anticipate that all the renovations might cost $20,000 USD, then you can assume that you should purchase the property for a maximum of $137,500 USD. If you spend *more* than $137,500 USD to acquire a home given these projections, you might end up with very little profit or none at all.

Single-Family vs Multi-Family Units

When it comes to flipping, there really is no limit or restriction as to the *kind* of property you can deal with. Single-family units, multi-family units, and even commercial units are all fair game in the world of flipping. But depending on your goals, you might want to consider some of the factors that make all of these choices *different*.

Single-Family Units

…as the name suggests are your typical single-family residential houses. They can fit one household and coincide with the idea of the *American Dream*. These are almost always the property of choice for flippers because they have the highest potential for a quick sale. According to a report released by the National Association of Realtors Research Department, an approximate 36%

of buyers are 37-year olds and below with small families looking for their first dwelling. Making up such a large chunk of the buying force, you might be better off targeting these individuals with SFUs.

The second largest demographic of buyers are individuals aged 38 to 52. Making up 26% of the market, these buyers are the ones most likely to spend the *most* on houses which means they're willing and able to purchase more expensive dwellings because they're at their earning capacity's peak. Making up 1/4 of the entire market, this demographic is another suitable target you might want to address by investing more in SFUs which are their choice of residence.

Multiple-Family Units

…are essentially multiple door properties that let you house several families at a time. Depending on your locality, there are different regulations that oversee the sale of apartment-like properties, but it is possible. Of course, most buyers want *single detached homes* that don't run too close to their next-door neighbors. Plus, if a person is ready to purchase, they might choose to extend their budget since just a few added thousands could land them a single-family unit.

Nonetheless, there is a market for these smaller, cheaper homes. The Silent Generation, making up 6% of home buyers, don't necessarily want to *invest* in expensive, large properties given the quiet, isolated nature of the lives they lead. What's more, they often want the security of a home just so they have somewhere to stay, so in essence, they'd be happy to settle with more affordable properties that just give them the bare essentials.

The market for multi-family homes can be much smaller, but there is a market. Does this bid well for your objective to fix and flip as fast as possible? Probably not since there aren't too many potential buyers. But if it turns out that you don't find the right purchaser at the right time, you always have the option to rent out each unit which can be a very lucrative and rewarding way to make a profit off of your property investment.

It's All in the Timing - When to Buy a Property

If it hasn't been made apparent yet, you need to know that the *timing* of your purchase will play a major role in the profitability of your venture. Take this scenario for example:

An investor managed to get a sweet deal on a $250,000 USD property in early February. Once the purchase was finalized, he got started on renovations which unfortunately took longer than he expected (a typical problem in house flipping.) He was able to declare the house sellable late in September with a calculated ROI of 13%. By then, spring fever had ended and buyers were back to their home bases, lying in wait for next year before making any property investments.

The house sat on the market throughout October, November, and December, getting one or two inquiries every few weeks. Many of the prospects would haggle aggressively, bringing the original calculated ROI from 13% down to just 9% - an unacceptable decrease from the investor's perspective.

Other direct home sellers in the area were much more willing to haggle since they weren't in the investment game and were truly more interested in liquidating their asset. So buyers during the off seasons found that there was no need to wait for the investor to engage in haggling since many other similar properties were being offered at lower prices.

By the time the new year came rolling around the corner, house prices in the area started dipping as part of the trend. During these first few months, the cost of properties around the investor's fix and flip were decreasing by up to 8.4%. Of course, our investor was yet again reluctant to make the sale. So he continued to wait for spring, when more buyers would be willing to pay more for quality homes.

By May of that year, the investor finally finds a suitable buyer for the property. Unfortunately, it had already been 15 months since he purchased the house which means that he had to pay 15 months worth of holding costs - including a mortgage.

So of his $41,000 USD gross profit, he would only actually net around $15,800 USD - assuming that the *income* tax that the government would impose on the profits *doesn't* exist. That means he only made $1,053 USD a month for 15 months. Now let that sit with you for a while.

In the flipping game, we're all prone to making mistakes. Sometimes, it's the allure of purchasing a property even when timing isn't right because you're worried you might not get a similar deal any time soon.

Unfortunately, jumping the gun and making that purchase without thinking about your timetable first can make for a lot of investment flops down the line. So it's vital that you take the time to figure out how long the entire process of flipping will take, including the amount of time your property might stay on the market without a viable tenant or buyer.

This also helps you map out exactly *when* you can have your property listed for sale. The benefit of knowing the precise month when you can actually entertain prospects is that you can effectively avoid low points in the real estate market, guaranteeing that you won't have to wait too long to get a serious bid.

Establishing Your Timetable

For house flippers, prospective investments are available and can be purchased all year round since these types of real estate offers don't follow the same *trends* that other properties do. You can find viable properties through auctions and foreclosures which generally cost less than the typical direct seller or realtor listings.

Now, since you'll always be able to find a potential flip at low cost any time of the year, the timing of your purchase doesn't really affect the amount you'll have to pay up front. What it does affect is the length of your wait before you can find a potential buyer for your property once it's up for sale.

The question now is - *how can you anticipate when you can prop up your property listing?* Consider this general timetable:

Buying the Property

<u>10 Days to 2 Weeks</u>

Once you've got your sights set on a property and you decide to go through with the purchase, then your timetable starts ticking.

Generally, you could spend anywhere from 10 days to 2 weeks to secure a listing, but that can change depending on a variety of factors. One of the aspects of the purchase that could reap profound changes on the length of time it would take is *where* or *from whom* you're acquiring the property from.

Renovating the House

<u>2 to 4 Months</u>

Some houses could only need a few cosmetic changes like a fresh coat of paint and new carpets, while others might require more extensive repairs involving the roofing, insulation, and plumbing. Depending on the extent of the required changes, you could anticipate anywhere from 2 to 4 months spent on executing repairs.

Will there be hiccups? Absolutely. In some cases, contractors might discover damages that weren't readily apparent, requiring that you mandate more renovations to make sure the house is livable. The weather during the repairs also plays a role in how fast it would take to get everything done. Ideally though, you won't want to spend any more than 4 months on all of the renovations since you the amount you pay as holding fees might exceed your budget's allowance.

Selling the Property

<u>1 and a Half Months to 6 Months</u>

Again, the time of the year when your listing becomes available will have an effect on the speed at which it's snapped up. For instance, listings that come up towards the end of the year might not see any potential or viable offers until the turn of the next year. It's just how buyers play their game.

If for example (and this is a *very optimistic* situation) you land a good offer within 10 days of self-advertising, you can then anticipate to enter escrow with your buyer. Depending on their choice of financing, it could take anywhere from 21 - 45 days for the purchase to be finalized. For cash buyers, it could be far shorter.

Assuming that there isn't a hiccup throughout the entire process, you could find yourself sealing the deal at the 90-day mark, ending your journey with that particular flip.

Given these estimates, you might spend anywhere between 4 months to close to a year holding on to a property you're trying to flip. Knowing how long this all might take and adjusting your expectations based on the size of the property as well as its sale-ability can help you come up with a rough estimate as to when you might be able to list it on the market.

The Ideal Target Date

So, what's the point in *knowing* all of this mumbo-jumbo if it doesn't really give you a concrete idea as to *when* a listing should be put up for sale? Fear not for the answer is quite simple - always aim to have your property ready for buyers by springtime.

During those spring months, the real estate market shifts from seller driven to buyer-driven as more individuals initiate the purchase without the need for sellers to inspire the need.

Spring is the *ideal* time for the largest demographic - 37-year olds with young families - to purchase because it gives them time to plan out their move before the start of the school year. Spending on a house at any other time means they might have to transfer their children mid-year, which really isn't an intuitive or practical decision.

What's more, diligent taxpayers can expect tax refund checks right towards the start of spring, which means they might have a hefty sum of money to add to their savings that they can use to spend on a new house. So this gives buyers more flexibility and a stronger capability to purchase.

If you're anticipating that a flip might take 8 months - including vacancy for rentals or availability for sales - you should make sure that those 8 months end right around springtime. This means that your listing will be up, ready, and ever-present as those eager home hunters seek out the perfect property to spend their savings and fat tax refunds. *Sweet.*

Decisions, Decisions - Where to Find a Flipping House

So you've got your budget and you've brushed up on all the things you need to know about choosing the right house to flip. *Thank you, internet!* Now, the only problem is… where exactly do you find these houses?

There are a variety of channels you can venture to seek out profitable property investments for your cause, and each one promises its own unique sets of pros and cons. Being the savvy immovable property pro that you are (or that you want to become), it's your responsibility to make sure all of these factors are taken into consideration towards the efficiency of your project.

Real Estate Agents

They say that one of the downsides of flipping a house is that it can be *knowledge-intensive*. For beginners, that can be painfully true. Because we don't all start out with specific industry knowledge that would have made it easy to navigate such technical terrain, there are times when you might find yourself in need of an expert. And who better to ask when it comes to property than a real estate agent?

Of course, these agents need to get paid and are unlikely to offer free services unless they're a close friend or family member (in which case, good for you!) So you would have to factor in the cost of their service to the expenses you make throughout the flipping process.

Nonetheless, these experts have *invaluable, dynamic knowledge* about the ins and outs of the real estate industry, and they might be able to share more than just information on the hottest, most promising potential investments with you if you're willing to buy them that extra cup of coffee.

Pros:

- Reliable, specific knowledge that's tailor-made for your needs and

- Unlock info on the *best* localities to flip homes in your area to cut down waiting time after renovations

- Get first dibs on listings that aren't available anywhere on the web or on ads from owners who go straight to realtors to sell for them

- Choices are narrowed down to your budget and requirements to save time from looking at houses that end up not meeting your standards

Cons:

- Services aren't free, and they're not always cheap

- Some real estate agents have specific ties that give their suggestions and recommendations preferential bias that benefits specific clients in their roster. Essentially, they might smooth talk you into buying a property that doesn't fully meet your needs because they have a client who wants that property sold asap.

- Get ready to have your phone ringing off the hook once you express even the faintest interest in purchasing a home. Hey, real estate agents gotta eat, too.

Wholesalers

You'd think that with commodities are large as houses, *every seller would be retail*. But quite the contrary. There are lots of companies and entities out there that take the form of property wholesalers - those who contract with home sellers and look for buyers before their contract runs out of time.

How does it work? For example, one wholesaler takes a house under contract at $80,000 USD. The house is a fixer-upper needing at least $30,000 USD in repairs before it becomes sellable to an actual homeowner. Once all fixed up, it could sell for around $160,000 USD.

The wholesaler looks for a possible investor (usually those who want to flip houses - a.k.a. YOU!) and *assigns* the original contract to that interested investor. He places the property at $100,000 USD.

This cost to purchase covers the cost of the original contract with the initial seller (who now turns the house over to you) and the middleman fee of $20,000 USD payable to the wholesaler who put you and the seller together. In effect, wholesalers sell houses and make a profit *without even owning them in the first place*. Isn't that something?

Wholesalers benefit two parties - the sellers who typically want fast cash and the buyers (you) who might be interested in profitable fixer-uppers as fast as possible. Of course, you need to be careful about that middleman fee which usually won't even be explicitly stated to you, leaving you in the dark about how much you *could have saved* had you gone straight to the seller instead.

Pros:

- Lots of viable fixer-upper projects served to you easy peasy so you can scan through and find a good choice within your budget in no time

- Really, *really fast* transactions that shave off precious days from your timetable

- Essentially a complete database of all the available houses for sale in a specific locality, saving you the need to seek alternatives elsewhere since they're likely all here.

Cons:

- Because the amount of money that the wholesaler makes off of the sale will *never* be disclosed to you, you might never know how much they've marked up the property from its original price

- They might have a completely different ARV appraisal compared to what you get from your own calculations

- It kinda feels a little scammy, doesn't it? Making a hefty profit out of a property that they don't really own? Hmm…

Auctions

Here's where you might be able to feel a little more *"pro."* Auctions can be blood pumping events where you battle it out with other interested investors over ultra-promising properties. Ah yes, bidding wars can be a major thrill ride! But there is a catch.

Sheriff's sales, estate auctions, and private auctions are a great way to get your hands-on cheap properties with exceptional promise and potential. Of course, you can find these listings published by the county weeks before the actual bid. Staying on top of these updates and scouting properties before the auction itself can help you establish an idea as to how much it might cost you and how much you can make off of it.

Keep in mind though that while you can view the property from the street, you won't be allowed to enter the premises or even look through the windows to see what's inside. So you're pretty much operating blind. If there are any structural issues inside the house that require significant repairs and renovations, that's a risk you'd have to be willing to take.

On top of that, there's the risk of *bidding wars*. While it is true that bidding against another aggressively passionate buyer can be fun and exhilarating, you need to keep your head on your shoulders. Losing sight of the cost you're willing to pay is easy if you're trying to *win* over another bidder. Remember - if you're paying *more* than your budget allows, you're actually *losing*.

Nonetheless, there are some pretty sweet deals in the auction scene if you manage to gain the experience for it. If you're not confident in your bidding prowess yet, don't force it. You can tag along to the event just to see how things unfold. There's also the trusty internet if you feel the need to learn a little more.

Pros:

- The cheapest prices you ever did see!

- Like really, really cheap houses.

- Did we mention cheap?

Cons:

- Beware of the bidding war thrill ride! Don't spend more than your set budget.

- Good luck with those surprise structural damages that you won't be able to inspect before making a purchase.

- No financing - only cash!

Multiple Listing Service

Ah yes, the information superhighway! They don't call it that for nothing, you know. If you've ever tried to scan the web for real estate listing, you might have already stumbled across the MLS - otherwise called the Multiple Listing Service.

The MLS is essentially an all-inclusive listing service that provides you with all the available properties for sale, categorized by locality. Properties can be new houses, foreclosures, or resales, and the listing aren't sponsored or commissioned by sellers. The MLS actually works with and for realtors, so it doesn't make money off of any transactions made between buyers and sellers.

The purpose of the MLS is actually to provide realtors a complete, consolidated list of properties so that none of them can *get ahead* of others with unlisted properties that only they have access to. This levels the playing ground for realtors in a specific locality, and makes sure that they have the equal opportunity to present *all potential* purchases to their clients.

Here's the catch though - the MLS doesn't allow membership to non-licensed realtors. So if you're just a happy house flipper looking for your next big investment, then you won't be able to enjoy membership on the suite. What's your best bet?

Look for a realtor who does have membership to gain access to the listings available. Otherwise, you might have to go off of the information provided through listing previews and guess your way from there. Oh, well.

Pros:

- All inclusive, extensive collection of listings that are easily categorized by type, locality, price, and a variety of other specifics to help narrow down your search efficiently.

- Latest real estate related news to help you catch up on updates and trends in your area

- Lots of great content to help enrich your knowledge on immovable properties

Cons:

- Requires membership fees of $100 USD monthly

- Not available to non-realtors

- At the end of the day, it's not as dynamic as hiring a realtor

Funding Your Fix N' Flip

Unless you've got a bit of money in the bank (and we're talking enough to purchase a house, pay for renovations, and shoulder any extra expenses that might not be apparent at the start) then you might find yourself in a bit of a pickle. How can you fund an entire flip all on your own if you don't have that kind of money lying around?

The answer is *you don't*. These days, there are lots of different lending options you can exercise in order to get the money you need to finance your entire project or a portion of it. Keep in mind though that these lenders won't give you money for nothing - they charge interest rates in order to make a profit off of the money you borrow. So you will have to subtract that from your gross profit.

Hard Money Lenders

Possibly the most popular financing option for investors in the fix n' flip business is the hard money lender. These entities lend borrowers a specified amount - sometimes the full amount needed for the project - and charge a steep interest rate compared to banks and other financial institutions.

The reason why they're the preferred lending options for fix n' flippers is because they're easy to approve and they can usually provide the full amount you need, so you don't have to pay for anything out of your own pocket. The downside? On average, a hard money lender will charge up to 16% of the value borrowed, and a 4% origination fee, which can be a lot to handle.

Equity Partners

Think of an equity partner as almost like a hard money lender - private individuals who can grant large sums of money to cover all the expenses associated with your flip. The difference is that these investors are also like "hands-off" flippers. What that means is that they *look for someone* who wants to flip - like you - but doesn't have the money to get it done.

The finance the whole project and you do all the dirty work, including finding the property, overseeing renovations, and closing the sale. What they gain at the end of it is *equity* - an equal share of what you earned. So usually, equity partners will get around 50% of the net profit.

If you have a close friend or family member who has the money to spend on a flip, then you might want to consider asking them to become an equity partner. The only gamble here though is that you can *never be sure* of the profit you'll make in the end. So if you only manage to make 9% ROI, then you have to split that down the line, no matter how small the end cuts might be.

In some cases, an equity partner might even ask for more than just 50%. After all, none of this would have been possible if not for their money. At the end of the day, you're at their mercy and your profits would be completely shaved down after everything's been said and done. But then again, if you're only just starting out, it does make a great strategy to exercise your flipping muscles with less risk and 0% interest.

Traditional Financing

Not a lot of flippers opt to go with bank loans because they hinge on your own debt status as well as your credit rating. If anything goes downhill, your credit identity might be on the line. Other than that, banks have a lot of red tape and often require lots of documentation before they can grant a loan request. This can weigh down on your timetable and prevent you from getting things started as soon as you want to.

Finally, you also have to understand that banks won't provide you just any random loan amount you ask for. They'll need to understand what you need it for, and will then valuate the property you want to rehab based on their own standards. This means you might only receive 65-75% of the value you need, requiring that you pay for the rest of the amount from your own pocket.

Well, that was quite a lot to digest, wasn't it? But keep faithful, oh eager flipper! We've only just uncovered the tip of the iceberg. No doubt, knowing *how* and *where to find* the right house to flip is the foundation of a successful and profitable fix n' flip venture.

But there's a lot more to it than just that. Over the next few chapters, we're talking about all the next steps you need to take once that property is finally under your name. So if you're ready for another intensive discussion, then keep on reading because it's time to get down and dirty - let's talk renovations.

3

Real Transformation Through Renovation

"Renovating old homes is not about making them look new - it's about making 'new' unnecessary."

- Ty McBride

You finally have your hands-on that sweet ownership title - congratulations are in order! But before you celebrate your success, keep in mind that the battle has only just begun. Oh, humble flipper - there's a whole lot left to do if you want to turn that title into profit, and it starts with your renovation.

Renovating an old home restores *value* because it makes the property livable and aesthetically appealing. After all - no one could ever see themselves living in a run-down shack! Buyers *gravitate* towards fresh coats of paint and clean new tiles, so it's important to make those changes if you want to reel in buyers without having to push such a hard sell.

Just like the home selection process, there are a few guidelines you should keep in mind when planning out a renovation. These key points should help direct you towards making the right choices, so you get the best returns out of your effort without having to spend more than you're willing to or capable of.

The Foundations of a Cost-Effective Renovation

Understanding what's necessary and what's luxury sets the boundaries and helps keep your budget in order. As a general rule, you'll want to do *the least* without sacrificing build quality and aesthetic. This will help maintain your project within reasonable cost and time limits without affecting its appeal to your prospective buyers.

Keep in Line with Competition

You probably thought that the first step to planning a renovation is doing a thorough inspection of your property. But on the contrary, the first step is actually scoping *other* similar properties for sale in your area. Sound funny? It definitely does, but there's a completely valid explanation.

Consider this scenario: you just got your hands-on a 3BR/2TB 1500 square foot home in a quiet suburban locality. Without stopping to check the competition, you order an extensive renovation.

You're thinking of painting it a new exterior color, landscaping with new trees and bushes to line the perimeter walls, switching out the wooden floorboards with marble tiles, remodeling the stairs, and giving the bathrooms completely new fixtures, tubs, and toilets.

It would cost you roughly $65,000 to get everything done. You call your contractor, tell them to get started, and watch the project unfold over 5 months. When it's all done, you have a fully renovated house that looks like a pretty picture ripped out of a magazine. Now, it's time to lie and wait for those hungry house hunters to snap up your listing.

Unfortunately, things don't really turn out how you had expected. It's been 4 months since listing, and you notice that there hasn't been a lot of activity. What's the problem?

Upon inspecting nearby listings of a similar size, you find that they're far cheaper. With the same 3BR/2TB provision and 1500 square foot land area, these houses are modest, yet clean and livable. They look decent and have a rustic charm with their wooden floorings and accents.

These houses have gotten quite a few bids over the course of your renovation. And what was originally 4 properties are now just 2 - with the other 2 having been sold since you purchased your home. Yikes.

Unfortunately for you, the cost you spent on the renovations will make it *impossible* to cut your selling price back unless you're willing to make just break even. If you do manage to push the numbers back a little, you might just have a few thousands left behind after you pay all the fees and taxes once you make your sale.

So, sadly this flip n' fix might be a bit of flop. The pitfall? *Not checking the competition.* The purpose of familiarizing yourself with other available listings of similar qualities in your locality is to help establish the aesthetic and quality that buyers will see in the area.

If your home looks worse, then buyers might be more inclined to purchase slightly more expensive houses to avoid the need to make any changes on their own. If your home is *too renovated*, then you might have spent too much to get your property to look *way different* while *weighing down its cost*. Sure, it looks bangin' - but with a far smaller budget, prospective purchasers can get really decent properties in the same area that are just as livable.

Essentially, what you want is to look even just *slightly* better than competition. You don't need to pay for such expensive changes that make you *exceptionally different* - all you need to aim for is cleaner and fresher! In a lot of cases, that could mean just allowing a few cosmetic changes to give your house that brand-new look and feel.

In Gary Caufield's words - *"I've seen gold-plated taps worth $6,000 USD each, or you can have the same water coming out of a perfectly nice-looking $60 USD tap. It's easy to get carried away."* Don't let the desire to create America's next most iconic home sway you from your purpose - do the least but be the best.

Know When to DIY

We're not all home improvement experts, so you will need to hire a contractor somewhere down the line... but do you *really?* Perhaps during your own home ownership experience, you've had to oversee a few home improvement projects on your own.

These likely ranged from simple repainting jobs, to woodworking and everything in between. Whatever the case, it was cheaper to get it done by yourself and a few subcontractors instead of hiring a general contractor to do the job for you.

Unfortunately, the decision to push through as a DIY contractor might change if the house you're dealing with is going to be *sold* for a profit. But then again, getting it done DIY means you can cut back on the cost and increase your net profit. So what do you do?

There are a few things you can ask yourself if you want to find out whether you're ready to take on the job of a DIY contractor. Understanding where you stand in terms of these factors will give you a realistic idea regarding your readiness and capability to oversee the operations yourself.

- Do you have the time and availability to be present on site throughout the renovation process?

- Are you comfortable working with your hands and getting things done using power tools, construction materials, etc?

- Are the repairs and renovations required within your set of skills?

- Do you have contacts with subcontractors to do more tedious, technical jobs for you?

- Do you possess some knowledge on home improvement and renovation?

- Are you confident in your capability to generate outcomes comparable to a professional contractor given the tasks you intend to do yourself?

If you answered *no* to any one of these questions, then you might be better off seeking a pro. Look - we're not underestimating your capabilities and it's true that everyone can definitely learn to get home improvements done DIY-style. But taking a gamble with an investment could mean more expenses down the line.

If you end up botching up any part of the repairs, you might have to call in a pro anyway and end up making extra payments for more renovations than you initially required.

Even if you manage to get the repairs done all by yourself, there's the issue of quality. Does it look like something a potential buyer would be happy to see and pay for? Or will it likely deter prospective purchasers? If it doesn't really improve the saleability of your property, you'd have to get a contractor anyway to clean things up for you.

Don't let the allure of saving 10% - 30% on renovation costs get the best of you - you should know what's best for your property! If you feel that you're biting off more than you can chew, you probably are.

Start with Bare Minimum

Remember - you're not aiming to create the next Better Homes and Gardens featured property. So don't go overboard with the changes you want to make.

Generally, if you followed the right steps in the home selection process, the layout of your home should be suitable enough to work off of without having to change anything about the blueprint - which leads us to a guiding mantra in the process of fixing a flip.

Focus on the cosmetic.

Nicked paint, yellowish grout, broken tiles, leaky ceilings, old bathroom fixtures, creaky cabinet and cupboard doors, and other features that might make the home *look* unappealing should be the focus of your efforts. These don't make any changes to the overall footprint of the property and are generally cheaper to get done.

If you got your home from an auction and you weren't able to give it a closer inspection before sealing the deal, it's possible that you might find a few structural damages when you finally get to walk inside.

Issues concerning windows, weight-bearing beams, rotten walls, damaged roofing, and other features of the home that have something to do with the framework of the house can be a set back in terms of both time and cost. It's also worth mentioning that these repairs typically require different permits before they can be started. So that definitely adds to the expense on top of lengthening your timeline.

Again, it's worth reiterating that the *house you choose* will be pivotal to the profitability of your project. Make the wrong choice at the start and you might find yourself scrambling to figure out whether you can actually make a profit at all.

The 4 Kinds of Home Renovations

There are 4 different kinds of renovations that you can execute on your property, and each of these increase the value and saleability of your investment. Understanding which ones you need will help you come up with a plan that maximizes your property's AFV without having to spend too much of your budget.

The Basics

Basic renovations are changes and repairs that address features that buyers *expect* should be in good order. Ceilings that don't drip and leak in the rain, functional gutters and downspouts, a working furnace, and other basic aspects should be in good working condition if you want to attract buyers.

You don't necessarily have to renovate them all to the highest of standards - simple maintenance tasks and a few minor changes to get everything working can be more than enough.

Now the question - does basic renovation add value to your property? Not exactly. Buyers expect that houses for sale should have all of these basics in order to be considered viable options. Essentially, making sure that all of your investment's necessary features are operational simply brings your home up to standards.

So, should you get them done? *Absolutely.* If your home doesn't have all of these basics properly addressed, then you might not be able to reel in any buyers in the first place.

Curb Appeal

These renovations improve the aesthetic appeal of your property. Again, they don't necessarily add value but they will help make your house sell faster. Investing in these changes can make your property look handsome and inviting from the moment buyers take a glance, making it easier for them to visualize their life there and hopefully develop an attachment that drives profitable action.

Renovations that improve curb appeal include a well-manicured lawn, fresh coats of exterior and interior paint, clean carpets, and other cosmetic changes that make the place look neat and appealing.

Keep in mind though that there are some *curb appeal* changes that might only really appeal to you. So instead of trying to flex your interior design muscle, try to keep it simple. Neutral paint colors, a tasteful backsplash, and plain, clean bathroom tiles with white grout can be better than trying to impress buyers with your taste in unconventional bohemian inspired design.

Value-Adding

Now we move on to the aspect of renovation that actually *improves* the ARV of your investment. These changes focus on the features of the house that make it easier or more convenient to live in.

For instance, houses with updated HVAC systems that are eco-friendly and energy-efficient are likely to save its homeowner the added expense of clunky, outdated systems. The same goes for ranges and range hoods that are more efficient at saving electricity and eliminating foul odors from the interior space.

Value-adding renovations can be expensive at the get-go, so as a beginner, you might think they're not necessary. But because these changes can recoup up to 80% of their value once resale comes around, they can be incredibly beneficial for your endeavor.

Remember to stay within limits, though. Even if these changes add value, you don't want to be too different from the other houses in your vicinity. If you have state-of-the-art everything and the houses around just scream plain vanilla, your home might stick out… in a bad way.

Preferential

This house would look so much better with a game room in place of that third bedroom! Before you *okay* the renovation, ask yourself - is this something *you* prefer or is it a change that would get the thumbs up from anyone and everyone?

One major pitfall that many beginners succumb to when flipping their first house is treating it like *home*. The last thing you'd want is to make the mistake of developing an attachment to your investment, which might push you to make decisions that appeal more to your own sense of "practicality" and "improvement" instead of the market's concept of ideal.

Again, the best way to stay grounded when planning out those changes is by checking out the competition. If most of the houses for sale in the area have 3 bedrooms and no game rooms, you'd be better off following suit.

Other changes that fit into this category include hot tubs, wine cellars, swimming pools, and ponds. Not everyone wants them, and some of them might actually be a maintenance nightmare, making them a downside for practical buyers who want a home that's not hard to live in or to keep in good condition.

Putting Together Your Dream Team

One of the best ways to make sure you don't exceed your budget with each flip is to put together a professional team. These contractors and subcontractors will be the people you work with even on later projects, making it easier to stay on the same page regarding the changes you want to apply to your investment.

Putting together a solid team of home renovators can be tricky, especially if you're not necessarily familiar with the most prominent workers in your area. So you do have quite a bit of a lengthy process in front of you if you want to make sure you're getting the best.

Know What You Want

If you're not necessarily a home improvement pro, you might find it impossible to know *exactly* what needs to be changed or renovated when you first walk through your home. What you can do though is inspect any cosmetic changes that you feel are necessary and list these to come up with a general idea as to what you want to do with your house.

For more technical improvements, you might have to call in a professional who can give you a more accurate understanding of the specialized changes that need to happen. An architect, designer, or general contractor can be a good choice.

Scout for Your First Member

It's likely that the first professional you'll need on your team is an architect or designer. These pros can draw up constructional plans and help you get a better understanding of technical problems that need to be addressed. On top of that, these professionals can also look for contractors and subcontractors who can work on your project.

What you need to know however is that these services need to be paid for. So hiring an architect or designer to oversee your project can put a bit of a dent in your wallet, especially if you're going with someone who has more experience and credentials.

If you're not sure which professional you should on-board, it's okay. This simply means that there hasn't been anyone who has appealed to your specific standards and preferences just yet. So instead of rushing in to the hire, you might want to consider scouting your options. Once you do that, you can get a free consultation with each one to find out how much they'd charge and what they think needs to be done.

In doing this, you can compare their recommendations across the board. Are they all saying the same things? Are some architects pointing out changes that others feel aren't necessary? The ones who say that *more repairs* are necessary might actually be pointing out non-essential changes that they simply feel like recommending to bump up costs.

Ask Around

If you still haven't made a hire, don't worry. There's no harm in making sure you've got the right guys for the job. Another way to help improve your search and see all the available professionals who you might be able to work with is to ask around. People in the area are probably more aware of the more affordable yet reliable contractors and professionals that can help you with your project. You can ask friends in the area if they can recommend anyone, and maybe even ask if you can get preferred rates since you're being referred by someone that got services in the past.

If you worked with a real estate agent to find the house you purchased, they might also be able to provide some valuable input. After all, it would work in your favor if all the members of your team were familiar with each other to help keep a smooth flow of operations without the issue of personality clashes.

Narrow It Down

Now that you have a few favorites, it's time to narrow it down even further. The best way to do this would be to seek an interview with each professional you've found to find out what they can do for you, how much their services cost, and whether or not you feel that your personalities would click.

Sure, you're not looking for friends, so issues with personality traits should be the last of your concerns, right? Wrong. Working with people you can't see eye to eye with can make the entire renovation process taxing, tiring, and downright difficult. As a general rule, you should want to *get along* seamlessly with the people on your team especially because of the time-pressured situation of a house flip.

Compare the costs of each pro and assess whether you'd feel comfortable with the ones you've chosen. If you think you've found the right ones, then go ahead and make that hire.

Negotiate Fees

If your chosen contractors and professionals have fees that fit your budget perfectly, then there might not be a need to negotiate at all. Remember, it pays to be fair - these people are trying to make a living, so it would only be right to pay them the cost of their services. But if you find that some of the professionals on your roster charge a little more than the others, then you might be able to negotiate a more agreeable fee. This should help keep you within budget without having to start over the process of seeking out a suitable replacement.

Try to ask your team if they'd be willing to agree to a slightly lower price. To make it easier for them to agree, you can tell them that you plan to keep flipping houses as a long-term money-making strategy. That said, you will re-hire them for future projects, giving them a steady line of work even during supposed off seasons for their business.

Smart Tips for Renovating a Flip

When it comes to the renovation aspect of your project, the name of the game is cost reduction. The less you spend to get all of those changes out of the way, the more profit you'll make once you decide it's time to put your house up for sale.

Here are a few more money-saving strategies you can enact to help stay within or below budget without having to sacrifice the quality of your renovation.

Buy Power Tools

If you're planning to go big with DIY, then you might be better off buying power tools instead of renting them. Sure, it might seem more expensive now, but they'll be pretty much with you for as long as they're working. So you can offset their cost over a number of flips, not just the one you're working on right now.

Other than the contents of your standard toolbox, you should want to invest in a circular saw, reciprocating saw, nail gun, sander, drill, heat gun, and perhaps even a power washer to clean out decking and siding. Make sure you don't skimp out on their quality as well - the better the tools you buy, the longer they'll last in your care.

Ask for Remnant Materials

Visit your local construction supply shop and you might be able to get your hands-on discounted items by simply asking the clerks whether they have them stored in the back. Some buyers can be particularly detail-oriented when it comes to their purchases, so materials that have even the slightest dings, cracks, or imperfections often get sent back and replaced.

Stores keep these items in the back and hold them off until sale season, but you can get your hands-on them any time of the year by simply asking if they have any. These materials can be great for small projects, and a lot of these lightly used items can pass off as brand-new as long as you know how to mitigate their damages.

Weigh the Importance of Each Room

Did you know that the kitchen, master bathroom, and master bedroom are respectively the most important parts of a home for most buyers? These rooms have to have the best quality finishes, and drive prospects to their decision based on the appeal that each room offers.

That said, you can assume that the other rooms - bedrooms, living room, dining room, and other areas in the space - are of less importance and simply need to be clean and livable compared to the primary rooms of interest.

What this means for you is that you can cut back on costs by investing in premium materials for the kitchen, master bedroom, and bathroom. For other, less important rooms in the house, consider shelling out on builders-grade materials. These are much more affordable and can hold up fairly well if they're maintained properly, so they can work for most markets.

Hire Freelancers

Whatever the task, make sure to check out the freelance market since there can be some pretty impressive untapped talent there. These professionals work solo and often charge their own rate, making them much more affordable than hiring through agencies and construction companies.

Remember, large construction firms have equally large overhead costs. The cost of rent, utilities, admin workers, insurance, trucks, and other monthlies can mean that they have to weigh down their fees to meet all of their expenses while making a profit. So while they can provide you with all the services you need in one go, they can also sap your wallet of all its contents at the same time.

What you need to watch out for though when hiring freelancers is their insurance. Make sure they have coverage that pays out for accidental injury. Otherwise, you might have to deal with those costs as well in case they end up hurting themselves while working on your property.

Leverage Freebies

A lot of construction supply shops out there are trying to keep it competitive, so some of them will offer you a free design consultation if you end up purchasing a specific amount of product from them. So before you head out to the store, make sure you've got an all-inclusive list of all the things you need to purchase so you can meet that quota and get the free consult.

If you can have an in-store designer come to your property for free to help you with the plan, you might not need to hire an architect (win!) which helps reduce your expenses even more.

Choose One Shop and Stick to It

One thing that holds true for construction is that you won't always be able to purchase everything you need in one trip. Things will come up and changes will be made to the initial plan, requiring that you seek more material when the project is underway.

That said, you should make sure that you've settled on *one specific* construction supply shop where you intend to purchase all of the materials as you move through the renovation process. Scan the available retailers in your area and ask them for rewards and loyalty programs they might have to get a better understanding of where you can get the best value for your money.

Some construction supply shops might also team up with specific financial institutions like banks so that you can get special rebates if you use your credit card to make a purchase. If you're sure you can make those payments in full once your statement comes in the mail, then you can enjoy lots of impressive deals and promotions that aren't available through any other payment option or shop.

Ask About Overstocked Material

Storage is a powerful retail tool that most shops want to maximize. So you can be sure that construction supply stores will do anything to try to clear out storage space and make room for new, more profitable items.

When you search through the store for the items you need, approach a clerk and ask if they have any overstock materials of similar quality. They'd likely be happy to provide you a few options, since overstock and outdated items often eat up a lot of storage space, making it hard to take inventories and to stock up on items that are in demand.

As you might have guessed it, overstock items are often sold at a fraction of their original cost, so they do weigh a whole lot less on your budget without really getting stingy in terms of quality.

Establishing the Cost of Renovation

What's the point of all this saving if you have no idea as to the actual, measurable limits that you need to observe? Establishing the actual cost of renovation should happen *before* you get started on anything because it all factors in to the profit you'll make at the end of the endeavor. If you don't call the cost before beginning repairs, then you might find your profit to be much smaller once you make your sale.

The cost of renovations change from property to property because each house needs different repairs and changes. One way to get an estimate cost on renovations would be to take 10% of the price of the house when you purchased it. This should cover everything you need to pay for in order to flip the house. So if you purchased it for $300,000 USD, you should expect to allot a budget of $30,000 USD for repairs.

There are more accurate ways to come up with an estimate though. And this involves familiarizing yourself with the cost of materials at your local construction supply shop. Pay a visit to your chosen establishment and bring a pen and paper. List down all the materials you think you'd need to rehab a property and get both high and low costs based on the prices you see. Take this information home and organize it in a spreadsheet so you can easily access the details whenever you need them.

Next, go around and ask a bunch of contractors how much they charge for so and so. If you need a painting contractor, ask what he charges. The same goes for plumbers, exterminators, tiling, roofing, window, and other subcontractors you might need to help with your property. Get a bid from each one by outlining the kind of work you need done, and compare their prices across the board. Also make sure to state that you're looking for **labor only prices**, and that you will be the one supplying all the materials.

Now that you have all of this information, you might be able to come up with estimates for the different repairs you need. For instance, if a bucket of paint costs $24 USD and you need 2 buckets to paint each room in a 3 bedroom house, you'd need 6 buckets costing $144 USD. The painting contractor might charge you anywhere between $380 to $790 USD per room, which means you could pay between $1,140 USD to $2,370 USD to completely paint 3 bedrooms in your home. In total, the range for a painting job could be $1,284   to $2,514 - labor and materials included.

Now you've got both a high and low estimate, what you want to do is calculate the average cost, which in this case would be $1,899 USD. Perform the same estimations with the rest of the renovations you need and come up with a total cost.

Take this table for example:

REPAIR	LOW COST	HIGH COST
Paint bedrooms	$1,284	$2,514
Replace all carpets	$2,000	$2,500
Retile bathrooms	$700	$1,400
TOTAL COST	$3,984	$6,414
AVERAGE COST	$5,199	

Keep in mind that the estimate you get out of this method will still be highly speculative, and it may change depending on whether you choose more expensive materials and labor. You should also factor in the cost of permits and other fees when calculating your renovation cost. Sure, there's no way you can get the numbers for sure, but doing this can be much more realistic than simply assuming all the repairs would cost 10% of your investment's price at purchase.

How to Stay on Schedule

Aside from the actual expense associated with the hires, labor, and materials of the renovation itself, you also need to remember that *time* will have a large impact on your profit. The longer you hold on to a house, the longer you'll have to pay for its expenses. If you hold on it for too long, you might find that all the monthly payments you made *completely* offset your profit or leave you at a loss.

So making sure that the renovations run smoothly and according to schedule is an important facet of securing your profit and guaranteeing a fast flip.

Establish a Time Frame

Before calling up your friend for contractor recommendations, before going down to the local construction supply warehouse to list down prices, before even asking any professionals for their opinion - you need a time frame. Making sure that you allot enough time for each task will help keep you on track towards finishing your project as soon as possible.

1. **Measure** - The first thing that needs to be done is measuring the home. With an architect or design specialist, visit the house and map out the entire space. If the previous owner has a ready-made blueprint, this can eliminate the need to measure all together. Make sure it's intelligible and accurate though, and try to get it done in 2 weeks.

2. **Conceptualize** - Now, with your architect or designer, come up with the plan for renovation. This includes *all necessary changes* as well as drawing up a new floor plan to represent the house after the changes have been made. Be as specific as possible to eliminate confusion later on. Give yourself 2-3 weeks to finish the concept.

3. **Budget and Finance** - This step entails getting all the necessary estimates from suppliers and laborers, and consolidating all of that information into one solid number to help you establish the cost of your renovation. At this time, you might also seek out financing opportunities if you're not paying for the repairs from your own pocket. Give yourself 2-3 weeks for this.

4. **Documentation** - Once you've got your budget in order, it's time to secure all the permits and paperwork you need in order to properly and legally complete your renovations. If you need to go through zoning, you might end up spending more time on this step than you want to. So be thorough and ask all the questions before you proceed. Around 3-4 weeks should be enough to complete this task.

5. **Construction** - This final step involves sourcing your supplies, getting renovations built and performed, and

making any necessary changes to the plan as you move along. Essentially, at the end of construction, you should have a house that's ready for sale. Of course, time frames can change depending on the scope of the repairs as well as the efficiency of your team. But you can expect to be finished with construction between 6 weeks and 3 months.

Be Mindful of the Time

It's important to make sure that you're always aware of the phase of your renovation. Losing track of time, or planning certain aspects of the repairs without considering your time frame can cause you to lose precious weeks and make your flip much longer than you intended.

As a general rule, the first thing you need to consider is *delivery dates*. Larger construction materials like certain woods, tiles, and other necessities might not be readily available when you order them, so your supplier might have to put you on a delivery queue.

Ask for the estimated date of delivery so you can be present at the property when the trucks arrive. It also helps to know when the materials are coming so that you can instruct your team to be on site so they can get started with repairs as soon as the deliveries make their way through the door.

If you run into unexpected repairs (especially structural ones - yikes) as you go through renovations, ask your local municipal office whether there's any kind of red tape that might keep you from jumping on those structural damages ASAP. If they say that you need certain paperwork, try to get those done as soon as possible to prevent delays and address the repairs as soon as possible.

Hire a Project Manager

If you don't trust your own capabilities in overseeing a home renovation, you might want to look into hiring a project manager. These individuals are equipped with the skills necessary to keep a project - like a renovation - running on the dot. Of course, they might cost you more now, but they can help make sure that you won't have to wait too long for those repairs to finish.

At the start, it might be better for you to seek the assistance of a seasoned project manager. But as you continue to learn and grow in your expertise, you might be able to take the reins on your fix n' flips more confidently, especially when you learn the entire process of the renovation, as well as the necessary skills to efficiently see them through to completion.

Be Decisive

Eggshell blue or sandy fawn beige? Red-toned mosaic backsplash tiles or cobalt blue with intricate floral patterns? Decisions, decisions! Of course, we can't help but be critical when it comes to our choices - we want this house to look as good as possible! But remember, what you're aiming for is a timely completion, not a Pinterest-worthy design.

If you encounter any questions mid-way through your renovation, answer them quickly. Don't take your time sleeping on minor details that won't really affect the quality of the build. At the end of the day, what matters most is that you completed your renovation up to code and on schedule - all those smaller details about color and style can take a back seat.

True enough, the renovation part of the fix n' flip process can be the most tedious and toxic - but it's also often the most fun! During this phase, you can test your skills when it comes to handling people and projects, and improve your concepts of what makes a suitable, sellable home. As you continue to learn, you'll become more capable of making lightning-fast decisions for later flips, and you'll be able to confidently see through a renovation with little fuss.

Once that's all over though, things start to get technical. During the next part of the fix n' flip process, you'll encounter some more industry-specific ideas that might be difficult to grasp for first-timers. So grab that cuppa joe and limber up as we dive into the cut-throat scene of home selling.

CHAPTER

4

From Fix to Flip - Putting Your Property on the Market

"In any market, in any country, there will always be developers who make money. So I say all of this is doom and gloom, but there will always be people who make money because people always want homes."

- Sarah Beeny

Take a good long look at the product of your labor - isn't she a beaut? Now, you'd probably *love* to just step in and take residence yourself, but that wouldn't help you make a profit, now would it? Remember, the object of the game is to turn your capital and hard work into a pretty penny, and the only way to do that would be to make a sale.

You've probably already given some thought to the sale process and wondered - *where do I even start?* Don't worry, it can be really confusing and you might feel clumsy as you try to navigate the real estate market. But there are more ways to succeed in making a home sale then there are to fail - so rest assured that you'll find your way around the market with a little more study.

Different Methods of Selling a Home

These days, the technologies used in real estate have changed and revolutionized significantly that sellers like yourself can utilize a variety of options to make it easier to reach your target market. Using a combination of these methods can help increase your coverage and lead you towards potential purchasers who would make suitable buyers for your investment.

Private Selling

Thanks to the advancements in internet accessibility, sellers these days can sell their properties by themselves! This method of sale is usually completely free, and lets you take full control of your sale as well as allowing you to communicate with potential buyers directly.

Aside from posting online however, private selling also entails direct mail that you'd have to execute by yourself. Putting up posters, handing out flyers, and putting up signages around your property should help draw attention - but it can eat up quite a lot of your time.

The main benefit of selling privately is that you don't have to pay any fees, and you get to control everything from the comfort of home or even your mobile phone. Then again, it can be very time intensive. That said, it's often the best choice if you already have an interested buyer in the form of a friend or family member.

Pros:

- No fees, unless you choose to join listing websites that require membership fees.

- You're in control - you get to decide what your listings indicate and you communicate with buyers directly.

- Lots of great real estate marketplaces online that you can use to extend your reach.

Cons:

- You need to handle all viewings, even for buyers who might not be serious about their intent to purchase. This can be incredibly time-consuming.

- There are a lot of "joy shoppers" who go online and inquire regarding properties even if they have no real interest in purchasing. Because it's impossible to tell whether a prospect is simply inquiring for the heck of it, you might find yourself spending hours responding to messages.

- Time-intensive - get ready to dedicate your waking hours to finding that perfect prospect!

Real Estate Agents

Hiring a realtor might be your best bet if you feel like you'd want to be a little less hands-on when finding a possible buyer. These experts can list your home in a variety of exclusive websites (like the MLS) and draw more attention towards your listing because well, that's what they do best!

On top of that, realtors also handle all the visits and viewings, so you don't need to make yourself available when a potential buyer asks to see the property. Realtors are also responsible for all other marketing strategies to bring your house to wider audience, including signages and direct mail.

Of course, the downside of hiring a realtor is the cost. These people can charge up to 5% of the final sale price of your home if they manage to find a buyer for you, so you should factor that into the cost of your venture.

Pros:

- Dedicated sales support to let you sit back and relax while your designated expert looks for a buyer for you.

- They'll handle all the viewings and direct mail.

- Ad placement on a variety of exclusive websites like the MLS to extend your reach and find a suitable buyer *faster*.

Cons:

- Up to 5% of your final sale price as the fee - yikes!

- They're no strangers to dirty tricks. Beware! Some real estate agents will only present your listing to a select number of clients to make a double commission. This doesn't do anything for your time considerations or your intention to extend your reach.

- You are at the *mercy* of their timeline. If they have other listings to sell, you can only get so much attention. If you want to make a quick sale, pay extra.

Auctions

Just as you might have visited a few auctions to discover possible houses for your venture, so too can you sell your investment through an auction. The beauty of auction sales is that you get your cash upfront, as soon as that gavel strikes the podium.

Sure, it's not a perfect method. First of all, you need to *pay* the auctioneer to set up the auction in the first place, which is yet another expense out of your own pocket. Next, you need to accept the final sale price whether you like it or not (if you chose to go with an absolute sale scheme.) If you want to opt for the reserve auction, there's no guarantee that you'd have a sale at the end of the entire exercise.

Pros:

- Immediate cash-out in the case of an absolute auction - you can be sure that a sale will be made at the end of the auction.

- No need to wait for buyers and have your listing sit on the market.

- No need for realtors or the tedious process of posting online and dealing with viewings.

Cons:

- You might not be able to sell your house for the price that you were hoping to.

- In the case of a reserve auction, there is no guarantee of sale.

- Auctioneers can charge between 6-10% of the final sale price - ouch!

Setting the Stage - How to Stage Your House for Sale

If you chose to sell privately which isn't uncommon of beginners, then it's important that you learn the art of setting the stage. *Staging a home* means dressing it up and giving it some personality so that buyers who walk in can get an idea of what it would look like if it were fully decorated and furnished. This puts the size of the space into perspective, as well as gives the viewers a little inspiration as to how they can design the space to suit their preferences.

There's a lot more to dressing a home than simply stuffing it with your own personal items. Quite the contrary, dressing a property is something of an art, which means you need to brush up on the technique in order to properly execute it.

Give It a Scrub Down

After the renovations, it's possible that your space might be dusty and covered in rubble from all the repairs you did. While this does scream "brand new," you don't really want to keep all that dirt around when the buyers come visiting.

Make sure to clean everything and remove all waste from the project. Rooms of utmost importance when it comes to cleanliness are the kitchen and bathroom. Remove all grime and stains from tiles and grout, and make sure everything smells fresh and clean.

Go Green

You can never go wrong with potted plants - unless you put too many! Accenting your space with a few greens can help make it feel homier and fresher, so it's always a good idea to put a few potted plants here and there to add to your space's charm.

A single potted plant by the front door, some quaint cacti and succulents on tabletops, and perhaps a few hanging plants out round back can help add a lot of appeal to your house for a minimal cost.

First Impressions Last

The first thing your viewers will see is your porch or front door, and that first impression *matters*. Setting the tone for the rest of the viewing, the facade of your investment should receive extra care if you want to catch the attention of passers-by and others in the vicinity.

Generally, you should remove any dated decorations that might make it look odd especially if it's a completely different season. On top of that, you don't want to crowd the entry-way of your home with too many items. A single stool, a potted plant, a clean welcome mat are all more than enough to brighten up the entrance and make it more inviting.

If you notice some stains on the decking or the floor right before the front door, then go ahead and give it a scrub or power wash it away to give it a cost-friendly facelift.

Get Generic

Often, first-time flippers use their own stuff from their home in order to stage an investment. While there's absolutely no problem with that, you need to know that any of your items that look *too* personal might not be a good fit for the staging strategy.

Remember, you want your viewers to be able to see *themselves* living in the house. If there are photos of you with your family plastered on the walls or sitting on tables, then it might give the viewers the impression that the house is being lived in and they're simply guests paying a visit.

Give your buyers the image of a home that isn't currently occupied so it's easier for them to visualize themselves in the space. Leave out the family portraits and graduation certificates and choose to decorate with generic images of scenery instead.

Keep it Free Flowing

People have a tendency to go overboard with furnishing and decorating because, well, it's fun! But don't forget that you want to create an impression to drive profitable action. Buyers are more interested in homes that look and feel spacious, so the concept of *less is more* definitely applies in case of staging.

Instead of bringing down every last piece of your furniture from your own place down to your investment, stick to just the basics. One sofa, a 4-seater dining set, a few side tables, beds for each room, and some rugs and throw pillows can be more than enough to give the impression that your home is fully furnished without having to suffocate the space.

Leverage Light

When it comes to staging, most experts agree that light should be your best friend. Adding an airy, spacious feel to your investment, putting light in the right places can make it even more appealing to buyers. So make sure to invest in good, bright bulbs in a warm tone to add a touch of coziness to the interior.

Other than that, you can also leverage natural light. Sunlight can make a space look lighter, brighter, and bigger, so avoid draping with heavy curtains that block out the sun. Light, sheer curtains that allow people inside to see outside also increase the visibility of greenery which is a great way to make a house feel more like a home.

The Illusion of Height

High ceilings are a surefire way to get buyers to fall in love with your property. But if that wasn't something that you addressed with your renovations, then you might have to fake it with the way you stage your home.

There are ways to fake a high ceiling, and these include strategies that use visual illusions with longer pieces that stretch the aesthetic of your interior. Long curtains that run from the ceiling to the floor, use low furniture instead of tall shelves and bookcases, and try to use lighter colors for *everything* instead of contrasting with dark elements like solid wood furniture and dark-toned rugs. This gives the illusion of continuity so that the eye is fooled into seeing that the ceiling blurs in with the walls.

Keep a Clean Lawn

The lawn isn't really an essential part of a home, but it does add to aesthetic. Remember that buyers like to visualize themselves in a dreamy home setting, and that includes anything and everything that makes their property look appealing - including the lawn.

You don't need to throw money on expensive plants, shrubs, trees, and flowers. According to experts, the best way to wow with your lawn is to actually *do the least with it*. Keep the grass cut, remove weeds, and water it before visitors arrive to encourage the lush scent of nature to come through.

If you're still trying to cut back on costs, you don't need to pay a gardener to get it done. Hiring neighborhood kids on the weekends to keep your lawn well maintained will help keep it in proper condition the whole time it's available. If you've got a green thumb yourself and a bit of free time, you can get it done yourself.

Establishing Your After Repair Value

Hey, what do you know? It's time for some more math! Don't worry, we're going to try to keep it as simple as possible, and at the end of the whole exercise, you should be able to figure out how much you'll make off of your investment altogether.

To get things started, it's important to discuss what the after repair value or ARV of a property *is*. Essentially, this number demonstrates the sale value of the house once it's renovated and ready to be sold. The purpose of knowing your ARV *prior* to buying a property is that it tells you how much you can spend on the house itself as well as the renovations without eating up your profit.

Some expert flippers can tell the ARV of a house at a glance, before any of the flipping process even starts. As a beginner, that might not be the case, and it's likely that you need a little more guidance and some hard facts to be able to come up with reliable estimations. That's why it's easier to estimate your ARV after you're done with the renovations.

Here's a basic formula to get your ARV:

ARV = Property acquisition price + renovation cost

If you got your house for $100,000 USD and you repaired it for $25,000, then your ARV would be $125,000 USD. Of course, that's still clean of profit, so you need to factor in an increase to figure out how much you can make off of it. But you can't just decide on a number and sell it from there.

Check out other properties in the area - how much are they selling for? Maintaining yourself within range of competition makes it easier for buyers to see your house as a viable option. Price it too high, and you'd be too expensive. Price it too low, and buyers might think there's something *wrong* with your property - "what's the catch" mentality. We've all seen one too many horror movies of happy American families buying in to a house that was just too good to be true, and no one wants to be the next Amityville family!

But there are some expert home flippers who believe that the best way to snag a buyer is to price yourself slightly lower than market value - just around 2% lower. If your home looks better or at least looks fresh after renovations, if it competes with other houses in terms of features (location, number of rooms, floor and land area), and if you're priced slightly less than the rest despite being a fresh listing, then you can expect a line of potential buyers knocking on your door.

So in the instance of the house above, let's say that the other similar properties for sale in the area are going for $150,000 - $175,000 USD. Pricing yours at just $147,000 USD (2% less than the lowest selling house in the area) gives you an edge without shaving your profits off too drastically.

In this case, you would gross $22,000 USD in profit. And based on ROI computations (which we studied in earlier chapters), that would put you at around 17.6% which is a *very* impressive ROI indeed.

But what if you don't want to sell at less than 2%? What if you want to push the higher limit of $175,000 USD and make 40% ROI? Of course, that would be entirely up to you especially if you chose not to work with a real estate agent. But keep in mind that the more expensive your property, the longer it might sit on the market. And the longer you hold on to it, the more you'd have to pay for temporary ownership.

And with that, it's time we talked about holding fees.

The Cost of Temporary Ownership

Consider this: your house is up and ready to be sold, but there aren't any buyers just yet. So it sits on the market for a few months while you wait for a viable purchaser.

During that time, it's your responsibility to keep the property maintained - that includes watering the lawn, keeping it clean, making sure the lights are turned on and off on schedule, paying for homeowners association fees, as well as taxes, and a variety of other necessities to keep everything in check.

So who pays for all of that? Of course, none other than you.

Carrying or *holding* costs are payments and fees that need to be made in order to keep the house from falling into disrepair or from being defaulted. As long as there isn't anyone living in your property just yet, you need to make sure to pay for all of these fees yourself, so they do factor into your overall expenses.

Utilities

The cost of utilities accounts for electricity and water. Of course, unless you're *living in the house*, you shouldn't expect these monthlies to weigh you down too hard. At most, water bills might only account for the cost it takes to maintain your lawn, as well as the cost of cleaning in case you hire someone who ends up using some water to scrub away certain parts of the home like the bathroom and kitchen.

Electricity costs will account for lighting, especially if you try to maintain some fixtures turned on to give the property some visibility even at night. During viewings and open houses, you might also find yourself having to turn on some gadgets, devices, and appliances in order to showcase the house in context to the people viewing it.

Homeowner Association Fees

In certain communities, homeowners need to pay association dues. These payments are used towards the maintenance and improvement of a neighborhood. Usually, these are charged monthly but can also be paid ahead of time such as on a yearly schedule at a discounted price.

If you're anticipating to make a sale within a few months of finishing renovations, then you can probably pay for the dues on a monthly basis. That way, you only pay for them while you're there and transfer responsibility to the buyer before completing the year. But if you think that you might take a whole year before you can turn over the property, then the discounted annual payment might be the better option for you.

Taxes

Property taxes differ from state to state, and they may be paid monthly or annually depending on your circumstances. In most areas though, these fees are collected twice a year.

Usually, property taxes are computed based on the assessed value of the house multiplied by your local tax rate. So if for example the tax rate in your area is 1.5% and the house you own is estimated to be around $300,000 USD, then you need to pay $4,500 USD annually, or $2,250 USD twice a year.

Maintenance

Of course, while your investment is sitting, waiting for a buyer, you need to keep everything in order. There will be viewings, there will be people passing it by, and it will *continue to be visible* even if it's not occupied - so it needs to look orderly. If your property starts to look like the house from Jumanji *after* Alan Parish comes back from the board game, then you might lose potential buyers.

Paying someone to regularly water the lawn, trim the grass, and clean the interiors will help make sure that your investment is ready for a viewer any time and every time. Of course, if you don't want to pay for those extra fees, then you can get it done yourself. Given that you have the time to get down and dirty.

Mortgage

If you paid for your house and the renovations through a lender, you'll have to keep paying for those expenses out of your own pocket for a few months until you finally cash in your investment. Unfortunately, these can be pretty hefty, amounting to over $1,000 USD every month.

Once a buyer does seal the deal however, you can use a portion of that to pay for your balance. However, for as long as that house is temporarily yours, you'll have to keep paying for that mortgage with your own private funds, which can make it difficult especially if you don't have a lot of savings to start out with or if you have a personal mortgage you're already paying for.

Negotiating a Sale

So, you've got a few buyers lined up and ready to make an offer on your property - three families all vying to become the proud owner of the pretty little 2 bedroom you've spent the last 8 months working on. What can you do to leverage their interest in your investment in order to make the grandest returns?

Wait for Their Bids

How much is each party willing to pay? While you might have already indicated a value to go with your property, it's rare that a home buyer will pay that exact amount. After all, everyone wants to maximize their money, so you might find that interested buyers will typically bid below your selling price.

Consider this: You're selling a property for $320,000 USD. There are 3 bids - the first at $290,000 USD, the second at $295,000 USD, and the third at $300,000 USD. All under your desired value.

You purchased this property at $225,000 USD and were lucky enough to have it renovated completely for just $37,000 USD. That puts your expenses at $262,000 USD. Selling at $320,000 USD means you can generate a gross profit of $58,000 USD - around 22% ROI.

Other houses in the area are selling for just around the same amount, putting your $320,000 value right smack in the middle of the price range in the neighborhood. Do you agree with the highest bidder? Or can you counter?

Counter the Offers

As the owner of the property, you have the option to counter and that's an important aspect of negotiations that helps make sure you're not selling yourself short. Some buyers actually have the capacity to pay more, and just offer lower prices in the hope of getting a discounted purchase.

With all 3 bids, you can counter at $310,000 USD. At this point, the third bidder is closest to your desired value. All you have to do is wait and see if they retain their original bid, if any of the other 2 bidders comes closer to what you're asking for, or if any of the 3 rise up to your counter.

A Few Nifty Tricks

In the game of real estate, there are some tactics you can try in order to make negotiations more fruitful and beneficial for you without having to really squeeze too much out of your buyers. Remember, you don't want to toss an interested buyer out the window just because they're bidding low. Entertaining them as they come gives you a fighting chance at making a sale sooner rather than later.

For starters, you can divulge that you have a few other buyers interested in making a decision. Maybe they're coming around to the property today in order to give it one last look before they settle on making a purchase. Whatever the case, they have to be on the brink of buying to give your prospect the feeling of pressure.

Now, whether or not this other interested party actually exists is entirely up to you. What you want to create here is the *fear of missing out*. If your interested buyer is really invested in your property and they really feel like it's the right house for them, they'd likely jump the gun and make a decision based on their emotions just to get their hands-on the house first - even if there really wasn't a second buyer in the first place.

In the case of the previous scenario, claiming that there are 2 other interested parties would be the opposite of a lie, and actually really describes the situation for the families involved. If they act quick and choose to end negotiations at your desired value, you can make a fast sale and they can get ahead of the rest.

Conflict of Interest

So, now that you've told your buyers about the situation, 2 of the 3 families have decided to meet you at $310,000 USD. The problem now is deciding which of the two you grant the sale to. In real estate, the choice doesn't rest on your own personal preference, which means that you need to weigh the decision based on the *more* serious of the 2. How do you gauge that?

Easy - *by requesting earnest money*. Earnest money is a tool used in real estate to demonstrate the good faith of the buyer. During this time, the buyer issues a partial payment (a value usually decided upon by the seller) to show that they're interested and ready to purchase the house in full.

Another purpose of earnest money is almost like a *reservation fee*. By paying a partial amount, the buyer wins the sale against other interested parties, and the seller will then hold the property off until the rest of the paperwork and processing can proceed.

How much earnest money should you request? That depends on you, but typically, the buyer should be able to pay for the fee from their own pocket. Which means it can't be anything too steep that they'd have to take out a loan just to settle the reservation. In a slow-moving market where the buyer isn't getting a lot of offers, earnest money can be as little as $500 USD to $1000 USD.

However, since there is competition, you have the upper hand to ask for something more. A larger earnest money value will make it easier for you to see which of the 2 bidders is actually truly ready to push through with the purchase. In this case, you can request from 1-3% of the purchase value. Given the above example, it's possible that you might ask anywhere between $3,100 - $9,300 USD. Whoever gets to pay first, wins the bidding war and gets to proceed with the purchase.

When There Aren't Any Bites

So, you've had your property up and listed for a few weeks now. Why does it feel like the internet is suddenly a ghost town? No hits, no inquiries, no viewings, just no activity. What happened? And what can you do to get the ball rolling?

A Bad Time to Sell

Remember, the real estate market is a volatile one. If you put your property up for sale at the wrong time of the year, you might find that there aren't a lot of interested buyers.

Most people are interested in making a purchase in the spring when they have more time to deal with the logistics of a move. Any other time might make it feel inconvenient or impractical, especially if they have kids that are going to school.

What you can do: Unfortunately, if this is the issue, there isn't a lot that you can do. Just wait for the market to pick up and try to rally your efforts to post about your property online more often. You can also try going all out with open houses, but keep in mind that interest might remain low simply because of the timing.

Minor Flaws

The most fruitful *payment* you could ever make in the process of trying to sell a home is *paying attention to detail.* But dad jokes aside, there's a lot to gain out of making sure everything is spotless and perfect for your buyers.

Buyers are *very, very, VERY* picky when it comes to choosing a property to purchase. Of course, if you were spending every last penny of your hard earned savings on a house, you'd probably feel the need to be particular with your choices as well. So even the slightest issues with paint, a slightly broken tile, and a poorly kept lawn might push buyers away.

As a seller, you need to be particular and pristine with all of your repairs and renovations. During the staging process, you have to guarantee the utmost cleanliness. These small and seemingly insignificant details *matter* and they can change your buyers' minds.

What You Can Do: Visit your property one more time and scan everything. What seems to be out of place? Is there anything that could be cleaner? Tidier? *Better?* Make sure the place is spotless before letting anyone view it. If there's anything that you think could remotely cause a brow to raise, make sure you fix it.

Location Problems

One fix n' flip horror story involved an investor who spent $275,000 USD on a house plus renovations, only to have it sit on the market for nearly a month with no bites. While some would assume it was an issue of timing, a nearby property just 500 feet away sold in a matter of weeks after being listed.

It wasn't a flip so it wasn't in pristine, newly renovated condition. It also wasn't as large as the other houses in the neighborhood - with 1 less bedroom and 1 less bathroom than our investor's property.

What happened? Unfortunately, being 500 feet away also meant that the house was closer to the main road without actually being at the heart of the traffic and noise. This made it more accessible to parents and kids trying to get to and from their home to school or work.

On top of that, our investor's house was slightly hidden inside the neighborhood. Having to navigate a few extra turns and narrow streets before getting to the address, buyers felt that it was "inaccessible" despite being just a stone's throw away from the recently purchased competition.

What you can do: Sadly, there isn't a lot you can do to rectify the issue of location unless you've got the power to rip that property out of its current address and slap it down on a better lot.

In most cases, investors choose to drop their price to give buyers better value for the money they spend. Of course, it could mean that you'd have to settle with much smaller profit. But unless you want to have your house sit on the market for any longer, then there really isn't anything else you can do.

Design Setbacks

Remember how we said that some design changes you might make could be preferential? That is - they only appeal to your taste. Buyers might not be interested in the same aesthetic, so it might be difficult to push your choices on someone who wants something simpler or easier to adapt to their own interior design taste.

In a lot of ways, you don't even really need to exercise any creativity when trying to think up a look for the house you've purchased. More often than not, you can get all the guidance you need by simply checking out the competition.

It can't be stressed enough how important it is for you to make sure your renovations take inspiration from houses around you. This is your *competition*. So they will essentially dictate the variety of choices (or the cookie cutter standard) that buyers will expect in that area.

Playing it safe by following suit will help guarantee that you don't step outside the bounds of what most prospective purchasers would consider acceptable. So if everyone's sporting black granite countertops against subway backsplashes and gray walls, then do that. Don't try to exercise your interior design muscle right now - there's a time and place for everything. At this point, what you're trying to do is to make a sale. And the best way to do that would be to be like the rest of them.

What you can do: If you happened to make a few design choices that are working against you, you have 2 options. The first is pay for a few extra renovations to have those choices erased and replaced with the neighborhood standard. The second is to try to dress your space in a way that minimizes the design issue.

With option 1, you stand to get an interested buyer sooner albeit spending more. With option 2, you run the risk of having them notice the uncommon design aspect of your house and having your property sit on the market for longer. But the decision ultimately rests on you and what you find to be the lesser evil.

Cutting Corners

The name of the game is doing the most with the least. But when you find yourself cutting corners to make a bigger profit, you might notice that it does have an effect on the saleability of your house.

Home buyers are particular and careful - they know *quite a lot* about houses even if it's their first-time making a purchase. You can thank the good ol' internet for that. According to statistics, 42% of home buyers go online to look for information on the home purchase process as well as the specific factors to look for in a suitable home. So don't think you can hide any aspect of your investment from these meticulous purchasers.

An HVAC system that's over 20 years old, a toilet that doesn't flush, a basement that's prone to flooding - they'll see it all. As a seller, it's your responsibility to make sure that *everything* is in proper working order. So if it'll cost you extra during the renovation phase, so be it.

What you can do: List down all of the essential features of the house that you skipped or skimped out on during the repairs. Now go back to your contractor and ask what you can do to get it done.

Poor Staging

Even if you've got a beautiful house to work with, it's possible to deter buyers with one fatal mistake - poor staging. Using the wrong design techniques when you decorate and furnish your investment can make it hard for buyers to see the property's inherent beauty and thus turn away as soon as they step through the door.

You should know that the stuff you put in the house will have an effect on its appeal, so be careful how you decorate. Furniture that's outdated might make the house itself look outdated even if it's not. Decorations that are too overbearing and loud might leave the wrong impression on buyers. Forgetting to take how the space *flows* can make buyers feel like a space is too small or perhaps awkward.

Less is definitely more when it comes to staging. Just add the essentials - pieces of furniture that can help buyers make sense of a space and how they can use it. Small decorations, framed pictures of flowers and scenery, and just enough greens can make a space much more appealing.

What you can do: Hold an open house and leave little questionnaires for each visitor. Include items that ask them how they feel the place could be improved. Read up on their feedback and try to incorporate the most relevant suggestions into your staging strategy.

Little Interest

It's a beautiful home in the middle of a gorgeous, ideal suburban community. Renovations have the place looking like a dream, and the price definitely isn't too unreasonable. So what's the problem? If you objectively think that you've got your hands on a great property but it seems there just isn't enough public interest, then maybe there's a problem with the way you're marketing your home.

Remember, the only way people will view it or visit your open house is if they know it even exists. If you're not reaching enough people with your posts and listings, then it could translate to poor outcomes when viewing day comes rolling around the corner.

What you can do: If you chose to sell without the help of a real estate agent, then you need to reconsider your posting behavior. Experienced home rehab investors post on websites like Craigslist at least 3 times a day, using different versions of their original post in order to appeal to different readers.

Other than that, you might also want to extend your reach by posting your listing on more websites as well as prominent Facebook groups for communities in relevant areas of interest and locality.

If you have been posting aggressively and there still seems to be a lack of interest in your property, the problem might be the post itself. Ask yourself - are these images giving justice to the property? Have I given enough information to spark interest in readers?

Most experienced flippers invest in expert photographers to take photos of their properties for them. Some even purchase professional cameras and learn some of the tricks of the trade to be able to do it themselves.

If you're working with a real estate agent, you might want to audit what he's doing. Ask about his posting schedule and whether the property has been advertised in the MLS. In some cases, sellers have found that their agent's request to make an MLS listing was pending for months before anyone noticed. This means they lost precious time waiting for responses on a post that wasn't even publicly published.

Nobody said it would be easy! In fact, for first-timers, it's really easy to fail at flipping especially if you weren't able to call the right shots when they had to be made. Keep in mind though that you *can succeed* with flipping - all you need is presence of mind, practicality, and a realistic outlook on what can happen.

On top of that, it pays to be able to notice a sinking ship before it all goes underwater. Spotting potential dangers to your flip before they take full effect can help you enact a few exit strategies that can save you from capsizing while still making a very impressive profit.

5

Other Ways to Liquidate
or Profit Off a Flip

"The fanatic emphasis on 'plan B' that professionals talk about is not a coward's fall-back system. It serves a purpose, a purpose that a strategist has envisioned and planned before the need for an alternate solution surfaces."

- Andy Paula

One of the primary realities that you need to accept when you step into the world of house flipping is that it won't always go your way. There will be setbacks, changes to the original plan, and detours along the way, steering you in directions that you didn't even think existed before you began.

While the goal of every fix n' flipper is to make a profit by sealing a deal on a quick sale after renovation, that's not always what happens. Sometimes, there just aren't any buyers. Sometimes, the market just won't agree with you. Sometimes, there's just too much competition.

Whatever the case, you need to be able to spot when your ship is sinking so you can shift to plan B to avoid any more losses. This way, you can still make a profit on your property and eliminate the need to dip into your own pocket to finance everything while you try to figure out where you went wrong and what you need to do.

When It's Time for Plan B

Forums on Biggerpockets are filled to the brim with first-time flippers feeling anxious and scared about the future of their property. *"It's been listed for 2 weeks without any attention! I'm freaking out!"* As a beginner yourself, these pseudo-horror stories might have you sitting on the edge of your seat, wondering whether your property is destined for the same fate.

But before you let fear take a grip of your heart, let's put things into perspective. Every house is different, and every investor is different! So as long as you continue to play your cards right, you might see yourself entertaining a few interested bidders in a few weeks' time.

However, because we all know the harsh reality of failure, it's only normal to ask - when is it time to pivot over to plan B?

Too Long on the Market

If you've had your investment up on the internet and other advertisement platforms for a while now, and still haven't gotten a nibble, you might want to try amping up your marketing efforts. Unfortunately however, there are some cases when that house will just continue to sit there without any attention.

The problem with having your house on the market for *too long* is two-fold - first, it weighs heavier on your pocket withholding fees. Second, it makes the house unappealing to the general buying public. *This ad has been here for over a year - there must be something wrong with this house.*

You should generally base whether your house has been on the market for too long off of your timetable. If you expected to sell after 8 months and are now closing in on 9, then it might be time to try something new. On the other hand, some expert investors extend their time frame to 1 year, regardless of how long it took to purchase and renovate the property.

Bids are Too Low

So maybe you have managed to get a few interested buyers here and there. Sadly, every time they tossed you a bid, it seems they just couldn't meet you where you wanted them to. The bids were always too low, and even if you tried to negotiate or put some of your nifty tricks into action, they would just hold their last bid and tell you that's as far as they're willing to go.

If you notice that *all* of the bidders are gravitating towards a specific number that just doesn't seem to meet your desired price, then you might want to inspect surrounding properties. It's possible that they found a deal on a similar house and are trying to see whether you'd be willing to go down that low.

Plus, since there are cheaper houses in your area with similar qualities and size, then it's not likely that you'll find someone who'll pay more for something that's essentially the same.

You Just Have to Unload

While we all want to go into this thing and make a profit, there are some cases when investors just find the need to unload and unload quick. For instance, one investor found himself in the middle of a number of flips, and didn't have the mental bandwidth to deal with another one.

So he sold the last acquisition at break even because he felt like if he had continued with it, he would be spread too thinly to be able to oversee everything efficiently.

Sometimes, it just happens like that. So if you feel like you just need to disengage, there are ways you can sell your house or profit off of it without going the route you intended.

Exit Strategies for a Potential Flop

There are other ways to free your hands of that property before it starts searing into your pockets and bank account. Will they be just as profitable as a sale? Not all the time. But they can generate you some income that could make it easier to part with your project without having to incur a loss.

Drop the Price

If you were paying attention when we did the math, you probably already know how to compute the profit you'll make off of a property based on the values you have on hand. It would be perfect to aim for an ROI between 10% and 20%, but remember, when the going gets tough, you need to make changes.

Compute your ARV and see where you would stand if you removed $10,000 USD from the price. Now put the property back up for sale with the new discounted purchase price. Don't forget to mention how it's now $10,000 USD cheaper.

If you still don't get any leads in a month's time, drop the price again. You can keep doing this as long as your above break even. This helps guarantee that you don't end up incurring losses.

Lease It Out

Maybe you found an interested buyer who isn't ready to make a purchase, and isn't eligible for any sort of loan from any kind of lender. But they're really interested in your property right now, and they want to buy it sometime in the future. Plus, they do have money on hand to be able to pay for a down payment.

Perfect. This means you can lease out your investment and make a few extra bucks now. Have them pay the down payment, then let them rent it out. Use their rental payments to cover the carrying fees, and generate a contract of lease so they have the option to purchase it later on.

Did you make a sale? Not right now, you didn't. But at least you have a steady flow of income from rent to keep everything funded for the time being. On top of that, you might have to refinance the house or ask your lender for an extension on the loan you took out on the property.

Put It Up For Rent

Here's a great opportunity for long-term, steady income. Lots of flippers who were on the brink of a flop turned to rentals to make money off of their investment, and boy did it work out for them. The beauty of renting is that you get to make all of the necessary payments for your holding fees, and you get to make a little profit on top of that.

Of course, renting out becomes a long-term gig once you do decide to start it out. So be sure that you're ready for that kind of commitment before you choose this exit strategy. What's more, you should know that the cashflows change when you decide to have your property rented instead. So it's important to know the math before you begin.

Essentially, you'll want a rental rate that covers all of the monthly expenses while leaving a little for profit. You can also leave the utilities to be paid for by the tenant, since the numbers will mostly rely on their consumption. What you want to cover is your mortgage, insurance, taxes, and maintenance fees.

Take the following numbers for example:

MONEY IN

Monthly rent: ………..$2,750

MONEY OUT

Mortgage: $1,400

Insurance: $100

Taxes: $250

Maintenance: $200

HOA:.............................$300

Net monthly income: $500 x 12 months = $6,000 USD annually

Now, is it what you expected to make after all of that fuss? Probably not. Is it better than nothing? Absolutely. Plus, when that mortgage is completely paid off, you can get much more out of the rental fees. You just need to train yourself to be a little more patient.

It's also worth mentioning that you can't just choose a rental rate and stick with it. Generally, the rent you can require should be based off of the value of the property. So rent usually runs from 0.5% to 1.1% of the home's sale value. If your property is $350,000 USD, then you can charge a monthly rent of up to $3,850 USD.

Sell It Wholesale

It rarely ever happens that a property investor will find a quick way to liquidate a property, but it can happen. In most cases, it's because of personal reasons or limitations - problems that need to be addressed immediately, so investments need to take a back seat or get out of the car all together.

Selling wholesale means you get nothing but break even. You end up having the money to pay off your loans and you get the freedom from the experience - you don't have to manage the property any more.

The downside of course is that you don't get to make a profit off of your hard work. If you decide to go down this route, you can expect an immediate buyer within days. So for those who really need to exit and exit quick, this makes the ideal alternative.

Before you even dive into that investment, you need to know that hiccups happen. If you prepare for them beforehand, then you can have a profitable exit plan before everything goes downhill.

Sure, there's no risk in buying a house... if you were buying in cash. If you got it on a mortgage, it's a completely different story that might need special consideration. Don't forget to formulate a few exit strategies if things don't turn out how you want them to - your future self will thank you for it!

6

The Makings of a Flop
- Common Mistakes to Avoid

"The first rule of business is to survive, and the guiding principle of business economics is not the maximization of profit - it is the avoidance of loss."

- Pete Drucker

All the choices you make between deciding to flip a house and finally making a sale (or enacting any other exit strategy) will determine the profitability of your venture. If you make any mistakes that you fail to address along the way, then it's possible that you might come to a loss.

That said, it's ideal that you maintain awareness of the things that could turn your flip into a flop. This way, you can anticipate them and adjust your actions and responses to mitigate the problems that could arise later on as a result.

Choosing the Wrong House

It was stated in one of the earlier chapters that your choice of property will be the foundation of your success. And that will always hold true in the business of flipping. Failing to make the right considerations when choosing a home can turn your venture into a money hungry nightmare, sapping you of time and resources, and causing you to incur a loss when all is said and done.

Unfortunately, it can be hard to detect a "bad" house right off the bat, especially if you're not experienced enough. Lots of properties look like great choices, and you might get a strong enough gleam in your eye to jump the gun and make the purchase because it *looked* like a good pick.

But there's more to choosing a house than just considering appearances. There's the issue of location, age, and specifications. Is it accessible? Was it built before 1978? Does it compete with other houses for sale in the area in terms of size and capacity?

Before you make a decision, try to imagine yourself living in that house. What might have seemed like an ideal place in the neighborhood might actually be inaccessible to main roads. What might have seemed like a great layout might be an interior design nightmare. What might have seemed like a cozy blueprint might actually be subpar compared to more spacious choices in the area.

Ignoring the Neighbors

Every flipper loves the satisfaction of working with a shabby shack and turning into a beautiful single-family unit for a budding couple expecting their first baby. But be careful - some of the ugliest houses in the neighborhood might be flanked by equally ugly properties.

Don't let tunnel vision drive you to make a decision that might be difficult to rectify later on. Make sure you check the neighbors too to make sure your house is in a place that people would want to pay good money to be. If the next-door properties look like run-down danger zones, then it might not be worth it.

Paying Too Much

So you found a great property in an ideal location - and you're really sure about this one! Not only does it compete with other houses for sale in the area in terms of size, it comes at a really reasonable price, too. It was probably *made* for you - don't you think?

You take out a loan and buy that house without making negotiations. You like it too much to lose your shot! So now it's yours and you go through with renovations. Everything proceeds without a hitch, and you're happy to put your property on the market in just 4 months' time.

But now that you crunch the numbers - uh oh. It seems something's just not adding up. What happened? Why does your profit look like your 12th grade bank account? You trace back the issue and find the root cause - you paid too much for the house at the start.

This is one of the most common problems that first-time flippers run into. Because most are convinced that those primary computations are purely *speculative,* they feel that they're unnecessary. However, just because they're inaccurate, doesn't mean they can't be used to guide those first few steps into making an investment.

Knowing how much you stand to make before you purchase a property is an important aspect of flipping. If you do away with the numbers at any given point throughout the process, you run the risk of reducing your profit and potentially even incurring a loss.

Before you make a purchase, make sure you've got your computations in check. Consider how much other houses in the area are selling for and use that as an estimate of your ARV. Then consider the cost of renovation, and weigh all the numbers together. The 70% Rule would be a very nifty tool to use at this point in time.

Poor Renovation Choices

When you renovate your home, you want to do everything *just right*. Bring it up to standards, make it *compete with other properties for sale*, but don't overdo it so that it sticks out like a sore thumb amidst the competition. Use other houses as a gauge and always check back on what those properties offer if you feel unsure of what you're doing.

If you skimp out on renovations and make insufficient changes, your property will end up looking like an outdated option compared to the others around it. This is of course, on top of the potential functional problems that it might have.

If you pay for too many renovations, your property will end up much too expensive compared to others, making it difficult to lock in a buyer especially because they have more reasonably priced choices in the same area.

Before starting any sort of repair or change, always, always, *always* make it a point to check what the others offer. Use their homes as a guiding light and don't step beyond what they offer even if it doesn't necessarily appeal to your own preference. This is about meeting the buyers' expectations, not satisfying your own personal renovation preferences.

Overlooking Permits and Fees

There's a lot more to getting renovations done than just buying materials and contacting a contractor. There are permits, fees, and other papers that you need to secure in order to get started, and they're not always that easy to acquire. Sometimes, it could take weeks before a municipality can give you the go signal, and that can easily eat away at your timetable.

Before you even start to purchase any possible investments, familiarize yourself with the process of renovation. Map out the time it takes to get certain permits, and figure out how much extra you might need to have in order to cover all the costs as they come.

Miscalculating Holding Fees

A commonly overlooked expense is the holding or carrying fee. These charges will continue to run as long as you haven't found a buyer for your home yet. So be sure you have some sort of fund to pay them off with if you're anticipating that the sale might take a while.

There are lots of fix n' flip investors who lose all their profit on holding fees, especially when they don't get to make a sale as soon as they want to. This can easily eat away at your own savings and bank account, so be careful. Factor them into your budget beforehand and make sure you have just enough to fund them before they get out of hand.

Using Standard Smartphones for Pictures

Tons of ads posted online, and not a single inquiry. What gives? Before you blame the internet, consider this - maybe your ads don't look appealing enough. Most newbies tend to think that it doesn't really matter. A good looking, decently located property will sell itself, right? Wrong. In any case, *you* are responsible for selling your property, and that entails taking the time when it comes to developing your advertisement.

Remember that 50% of buyers will start with the web when in search of a home to purchase. So make the most of these platforms so they work in your favor. Expert flippers will even hire a professional photographer to compose shots and perform post-process to generate high-quality images that just rake in new leads. Of course, we might not all have that kind of budget, but it does pay to be particular with your listings.

If you can't hire a professional photographer, at least try to learn a few tricks to be able to capture high-quality photos. These can change the way your ads perform and may even bring a serious buyer to your doorstep sooner rather than later.

Not Posting Enough

If you were hoping to gain traction with that one Facebook post you published on your profile, you've got another thing - or absolutely *nothing* - coming. The purpose of online posting is extending your reach to people you wouldn't be able to reach any other way. There are people in neighboring states or even other countries who are looking to move in where your property is located - how can they find out about your house if you're not extending your visibility?

You can't just post once on Facebook or Zillow and be done with it. There's a benefit to continuously updating your listings. Newer listings often get indexed first, and that gives you the advantage of being seen before any other choices on a list.

So aside from posting on real estate websites, consider joining Facebook groups where you might find interested buyers. On top of that, it's also vital that you post *regularly* even if that means posting the same ads over and over again.

You never know who might be scanning those search results *now* - you might reach a completely new batch of viewers if you post today compared to those that you reached yesterday.

It also helps to reword your listings as you post them. You'll notice that words like "NEWLY RENOVATED" and "SPACIOUS" might receive more attention than headlines that use bland words.

Keep it interesting and write in a way that would encourage others to click your link and learn more about your post.

Fitting Everything Into an Unreasonable Timetable

There's beauty in achieving a quick flip, but there's no need to force it. While we all want to be able to make a sale as soon as possible, there's something to be gained out of taking your time where it's necessary.

Buyers these days are exceptionally meticulous, and they'll even call in experts to tell them what they don't know. So if you're trying to hide a few flaws in your home, hoping that they go unnoticed, you should know that they will definitely be seen.

Instead of trying to force a timetable that's just too short, allot time where you feel it's necessary. Don't pressure your contractors to get the job done faster, but try to make sure that they're not taking more time than they need.

Make sure all of the changes that need to be done are completed properly and appropriately. This way, you can snag a sale sooner instead of having to go back and forth trying to fix things you thought you could skip.

Pushing Plan A

We all love a guy (or gal!) who can stand her ground. But there is a time when it becomes impractical and just downright, well - stupid. A major concept you need to accept is that not all flips will go your way. Some will exceed your expectations and work out better than you thought, and others will completely drive you insane, wishing you had stuck to your day job instead.

Acknowledging that plans change even when you don't want them to will make it easier for you to switch to plan B when things start to go downhill. But if you choose to believe in your primary plan, if you think it can still work out and you just need a little more faith even if all the signs are telling you to disengage, then we've got a problem.

There's a lot to lose if your flip starts turning into a flop, and you need to be ready to switch gears when that happens. Remove your emotions from the situation and try to see things objectively. Emotional attachment to a venture is the leading cause of loss.

Paying Full for Materials

There are tons of budget-friendly options out there that can help you maximize your resources when buying supplies for the renovations. So don't shell out double the cost on materials that are of similar quality. Remember, in a lot of ways, retail is mostly about brands. Certain brands cost more than others, despite being exactly the same.

Exercise your shopping muscle when looking for discounted construction materials and always ask for alternatives to anything you find on the shelves. The odds are, those store clerks probably have something stored in the back that meets your needs without having to cost too much.

You might also want to check your credit cards for possibly rebates and rewards. Buying all of your supplies using these cards can give you access to exclusive offers and discounts that might not help with the construction per se, but still give you better value for the money you spend.

Avoiding the Experts

Sure, hiring a few extra professionals to help you out with your cause might cost you more now, but if you're really unsure how to get things done, then is there really any other choice? As an investor, there's something to gain out of being humble and practical enough to seek help when you know you're at a loss.

If you feel like you're having trouble figuring out the design for your house, call in an architect. If you can't DIY anything for the project, have the contractors do everything. If you're worried you might not be able to find a suitable buyer in time, ask a realtor to help you out.

Yes, it will cost you money to hire these people and ask them for their expertise. But at the end of the day, you can feel confident that you didn't skimp out on your project and that you have someone who knows what they're doing with your property. This doesn't only secure its ARV, but also helps ascertain that you won't have to wait for a buyer too long after making a listing.

Underestimating Staging

This is a good looking house, I don't really need to do a lot with it. For some people, staging can be fun and interesting. But for others (mostly men), it can be a tedious chore. No one wants to spend their time decorating a space that's not even theirs. Besides, if a house is good enough, it will pretty much sell itself.

Unfortunately, there's a lot to gain out of staging and sellers who don't leverage its inherent benefits run the risk of losing prospects and having their property sit on the market for way too long.

The purpose of staging is to paint a picture for your buyers. *This is what you can do with this property. This could be how you live.* It makes sense of a space and puts context. It makes it easier to see how your own life can unfold in a place you've never seen before. It taps into emotions - a powerful driving force in the realm of purchasing property.

If you don't want to go through the challenge of staging a house, try hiring someone to do it for you. There are countless home stagers out there who charge a minimal fee to help you dress your house up and sell it to prospects. In some cases, your real estate agent might already be offering that service for the amount that you pay them. Make sure to ask about it before you stage to find out how they can be of assistance.

Thinking It's a One-Man Job

While you might be the brains of this outfit, you need to recognize the indispensable role of the other people who are a part of your team. Your contractors, your agents, architects, and everyone else involved in the process is as much a part of the project as you are. So don't think you can do it all on your own.

A lot of times, newbies feel the need to micromanage their projects, assuming it's the best way to meet their goals and make a profit. But when it comes right down to it, these professionals probably know more about the industry than you do. So don't try to dictate how they should get their job done.

Trust the people you have on your team, learn from them, and make sure they get to provide their opinion especially if they're giving one on a topic that they're particularly knowledgeable about. After all, that's what you hired them for in the first place, right?

Spitballing the ARV

There are a lot of ways you can come up with the figures to represent your ARV. For instance, you can visit the neighborhood and check out the prices for other houses for sale. You can go online and see how much the houses in the area are selling for in general. You can base it off of the purchase price you got your property for, and see how all the cost of renovations can factor in to give you an idea of how much you can sell it for once it's all done.

While these all give you some idea as to the ARV of your property, none of those numbers can be certain. So it's always best to seek out a real estate agent who can help you develop a more accurate idea of what you can expect when you make a sale. The importance of knowing your ARV is that it can guide you as to the expense you can incur without eating up all your profit.

Don't make mistakes with those initial calculations, and if you can, find someone who can give you the most accurate estimations to help your project along the way to reasonable profit.

Doing Eraser Math

What a great piece of property! I wonder how I can make it fit my budget? If you find yourself having to ask that question in the first place, you might be better off looking elsewhere. Eraser math can be a deadly pit that can cause you to feel financially capable when you actually aren't.

For instance, some newbies will erase original anticipated ARVs and renovation fees in order to bump up their maximum purchase price. Sure, it might make your project seem like a financially sound opportunity on paper, but changing up the ARV in your logbook won't change it in real life.

Once you finally have your listing up, you'll find that it *won't* sell for your imaginary ARV because that's precisely what it was - an imaginary number you came up with just so you could get your hands on a property you really liked.

Stick to the numbers and trust the computations. Don't try to bend or flex the calculations just to make ends meet - you'll be thankful for it.

Making Your Savings a Part of the Equation

We've all heard those stories - people flipping houses without having a dime to their name. Once you do start flipping though, you'll realize the harsh reality that pocket money is something you have to have if you want to rehab properties.

While a lot of your expenses will be funded by a financing entity or a loan, you need to know that you will spend some of your money on the venture. Unexpected fees, repairs, permits, and other unforeseen charges can require you to pay for certain values out of your own pockets - and that's okay.

What's important is making sure you set limits. Unless you plan to fund everything from your own personal accounts, it's imperative that you list down all the times you paid for something with your own money. This helps make it easier to understand where profit ends and losses begin.

Failing to factor in the money you spent from your own savings could make it hard to detect whether you've made a profit at all. For instance, some flippers think they made *this much* when in fact, they only really made a fraction because they forgot to list down the times they spent on things from their own wallet.

On top of that, putting a limit on the amount you're willing to pay for yourself saves you from the danger of losing everything you have to your project. Of course, we all want to see our hard work come up with something good, but if it means shelling out everything you have, then you might want to look into a plan B.

Forgetting the Buyers

It's easy to get carried away when you're dealing with a renovation. You have color preferences, interior design inspiration, and lots of other concepts you want to try out to create a space that's uniquely *you*.

Unfortunately, developing a space that caters to your taste means you might end up forgetting what the buyers want to see. For the most part, people who are interested in purchasing a property want a space that looks clean, that's functional, and that can be easily adapted to their preferred interior design style.

If you incorporate too many factors that cater to your unique preferences, then it might be difficult for your buyers to see themselves in that space. So instead of letting your desire to design get the best of you, stick to the status quo. Follow what other houses for sale in the area have to offer. Don't stray too far. At the end of the day, plan vanilla sells.

Believing Too Strongly In Your Property

We all have the tendency to trust our own. It's just our natural disposition to feel proud of what's ours. So when you look at your property, you might be thinking, *wow, this here's a real masterpiece.*

While it's true that it might look like a real winner, you have to keep your expectations in line. Not everyone will see your property the same way because they weren't there when all the blood, sweat, and tears came pouring down. There will be low ballers and buyers who will look and scoff - it's all part of the process.

What you don't want is to let your belief in your property to dictate your decisions. If it feels like you're not getting the attention you deserve, or if you're struggling to make a sale, it might be time to bring down that selling price. While you might think your investment should be worth its weight in gold, the market probably doesn't and that's just the harsh reality.

Losing Sight of Time

First-time flippers often get caught up in the renovation process that they end up taking their sweet time. Sure, we all want to make the best out of what we have. But if that means shaving off significant amounts of time, then you should reconsider your strategy.

Losing sight of your timetable can make it very possible to exceed your designated time limit. If you reach your hard money loan due and you're still just wrapping up the repairs, then you've got yourself a problem.

Other than that, the time you spend rehabbing your property will dictate how much you'll have to pay in terms of holding fees. The longer you hold on to the house, the longer you extend your temporary ownership. In the long run, this could sap you of any profit and even cause a loss.

Establish a sound timetable before you start your project and make sure everyone on your team has a copy. Keep it somewhere visible and try to get updates from everyone to find out which part of the process they're currently working on. This should help keep everything in order and prevent your team from exceeding the allotted time.

Is this an all-inclusive list? Quite the contrary. There are a lot of other mistakes you could make - newbie or not. So it's important to read up and audit *yourself* throughout the entire process of the flip. The best way to avoid these issues to stay on top of operations and keep your eyes open in case of any potential problems.

There's no way to really eliminate risk 100% if you're flipping. And a lot of the decisions you make will rely on your foresight. Give yourself some time to learn and don't avoid the professionals - they're there to offer you knowledge and assistance. As you grow into your craft, you can start taking on more of the responsibilities to cut the cost without harming the outcomes of your endeavor.

Conclusion

Ah, the old fix and flip. It can be a very lucrative business venture. Lots of hopeful property investors have tried their hand at this exciting real estate exercise, and countless have succeeded in transitioning from their boring 9 to 5's in exchange of a life of flipping.

Is there anything stopping you from becoming a successful flipper? Perhaps the biggest obstacle in the way of any real estate rehab beginner is the fear of striking out. Any sort of apprehension, anxiety, nervousness, or fear can cause you to make the wrong decisions along the line, crippling your profit and causing your venture to crash and burn.

If there's anything you need to take away from this guide it's that house flipping needs your whole confidence and resolve. You need to be dedicated, you need to be committed, and you need to be aware of the risks in order to make sound decisions even during times of potential failure.

Will you fail? Let's be real - *you might*. That's a danger that you have to face. But if you're brave enough to see it through, you might just be staring at your next million-dollar enterprise.

So, to set you off on your way to your first flip, take these words from Giovanni Fernandez, the owner and CEO of National Real Estate:

"Everyone can invest in average opportunities; wealth is built by investing in the greatest opportunity the economy presents."

Remember, there are risks and potential downward spirals in every market. You *get ahead* by choosing a market that poses the least risk while offering the most gain.

When you flip houses, you're essentially buying and owning properties for short periods of time. And anyway you look at it - homeownership is an asset. As long as you have land, you stand the chance to make a profit. And that's a very powerful place to be.

Now, go, humble house flipper. And find your first profitable property in the great beyond.

Made in the USA
Middletown, DE
06 August 2019